KEEPING THE BEAT
What Count Basie Taught Me About Music, Mentorship and Leadership

DENNIS ROWLAND

A MEMOIR BY DENNIS ROWLAND
WITH MARLA SHEINER

A portion of proceeds supports music student scholarships.

Published by Sheiner Enterprises LLC

Printed in the United States of America

First Edition

ISBN 979-8-218-94601-2

Library of Congress Control Number 2026902003

Cover Photo Credit: Dan Vermillion , Herberger Theater Center, 2007

Book Design & Cover Miriam Contreras – Alphagraphics Camelback

www.MarlaSheiner.com

Contents

For

Count Basie—
a master of swing,
a model of restraint,
and proof that the strongest leaders
often say the least.

May these stories pass along
what he gave so freely.

Acknowledgements

First and always, my deepest gratitude is to my wife, Sydney, who has shared this life with me since our marriage in 1995. She has been my partner in every sense—steady, perceptive, and unfailingly generous in spirit. When my life and music were interrupted by a stroke many years ago, Sydney stood beside me with resolve and grace, advocating for me when needed and believing in my return long before it felt certain. Her faith, patience, and quiet strength carried me through that chapter and every one that followed. Without her, none of this would have been possible.

I am grateful as well to the teachers, mentors, bandleaders, and fellow musicians who shaped me—who trusted me with the music, challenged me to listen more deeply, and showed me what it means to serve something larger than oneself. In jazz, nothing is ever owned outright; it is carried, cared for, and passed along, shaped by those willing to honor its history while keeping it alive in the present. To the students who kept me curious and accountable, the colleagues who welcomed me into their bands and classrooms, and the friends who offered encouragement at just the right moments: you are all part of this story.

I also extend my thanks to the medical professionals and therapists who helped me regain my footing when the path forward was uncertain, and to the broader community that reminded me—through music, fellowship, and shared purpose— why returning mattered.

This book reflects not just my journey, but the generosity of a life spent in music with others. I am grateful for every note, every lesson, and every hand extended along the way.

Dennis Rowland
Phoenix, Arizona

~~~
~~~

As the writer and collaborator on this project, I am deeply grateful to Dennis for the generosity of his time, trust, and lived experience, all of which made this book possible. He opened his life, his work, and his memories with candor and care, and his willingness to reflect—honestly and without pretense—gave this story both its depth and its heart.

This work was shaped through long hours of independent research, immersed in jazz history, archival recordings, library collections, and the words of those who have written thoughtfully about this music and its makers. Like the music itself, this book rests on a continuum of knowledge passed forward, and I am especially appreciative of the librarians, historians, journalists, and chroniclers whose scholarship formed the foundation beneath these pages.

I am also grateful to those who helped bring this book into physical form, from design through production, and to the professionals whose skill and care ensured the work was treated with the respect it deserves. Finally, I thank the friends, colleagues, and loved ones who supported this project with patience and encouragement as it took shape.

This book is the result of shared effort—of listening closely, asking careful questions, and honoring a story worth preserving. I am thankful to all who played a part in bringing it into the world.

Marla Sheiner
Phoenix, Arizona

Authors' Notes

It started with a sweatshirt and a sandwich.

It was the holiday season of 2024, and I was standing in line at Bertha's Café, waiting for my order. Behind me, a man wearing a Kentucky State sweatshirt caught my eye. As one does when idling in a café line—with time to spare and a nose for a good story—I turned and said, "So… Kentucky State?"

He smiled. "Yeah."

"About when?" I asked, hoping I wasn't trespassing on the calendar.

"The late '60s."

"Well imagine that," I said, winking. "I went to Tempe Normal School back in the day—and I remember those days just fine." I added that I had a friend in Kentucky, which made us practically related. He laughed.

"What did you study at Kentucky State?" I asked as the line moved forward.

"Music."

The obvious follow-up came naturally. "So… did you use it?"

He paused, turned toward me, and said—quietly, plainly, without flourish—"Well, I'm a jazz singer."

Something in the tone stopped me. The phrasing. The humility. The absence of self-advertising. It all pointed to someone I had heard, seen, read about, and admired for years.

With a knowing smile, I asked softly, "Is your name Dennis?"

"Yes."

"And your last name... Rowland?"

"Yes."

Time stood still—at least for me. Just like that, the pieces clicked into place. I was standing in line with Dennis Rowland—former vocalist with the Count Basie Orchestra, a Phoenix treasure, and a deeply respected mentor to generations of musicians.

We introduced ourselves properly, shook hands, and went our separate ways—only to discover that we were both regulars. Over time, smiles turned into conversation, and neighboring café tables became places where real dialogue unfolded—often over ham-and-cheese sandwiches.

From the start, my curiosity was insatiable due to my professional background in mass communications. I spent five decades in journalism, communications, and brand management—asking questions, shaping narratives, assessing reputations, and knowing when a story mattered. That instinct lives in my bones.

What intrigued me about Dennis wasn't just what he had done, but how he had done it. To what extent does a place make a man? And how does a man, in turn, rise from that place with grace, discipline, and generosity intact?
As Dennis spoke, I felt something familiar: the responsibility to listen carefully—and, with permission, to share what

mattered. I had a journalist's instinct that I was to serve the public interest; to collect and disseminate a historical record yet untold. That Bertha's Café brought us together felt more than coincidental. More than a chance meeting. To me, it felt as if I had been assigned a duty at a site where I was to serve the greater good.

Eventually, I worked up the nerve to ask, "Would you mind if I recorded some of this? Maybe I'll transcribe it some-day—stitch it together like a patchwork quilt."

He agreed without hesitation. And just like that, this book began.

Keeping the Beat is Dennis's story, told in his voice—born at a corner café and shaped by music, memory, and lived experience. It is not a strict chronology, but a collection of moments that reveal how Dennis Rowland has navigated a remarkable life: from Detroit to the world stage, from Basie's bandstand to Phoenix classrooms, from ambition to mentorship.

These pages reflect my deep belief that Dennis Rowland— our star historian—has something enduring to teach us about craft, leadership, and how to live well in rhythm with others.

Marla Sheiner
Phoenix, Arizona

~~~

People often ask me when I knew music would be my life.

The truth is, I didn't think about it that way—not then, and not even now. I just kept saying yes to the next note, the next opportunity, the next person who believed in me enough to listen.
~~~

When Marla and I first started talking at Bertha's Café, I didn't imagine those conversations would turn into a book. They felt like what they were: two regulars talking about life, music, Detroit, teachers, bandstands, and the long road that turns talent into craft. What surprised me was how carefully she listened—and how much she understood about stories, context, and responsibility.

I've spent my life learning from great musicians, great mentors, and great rooms. From Detroit to Kentucky State, from the Count Basie Orchestra to classrooms and stages in Phoenix, I've been shaped by people who showed me how to lead without raising your voice, how to serve the music, and how to leave space for others to shine.

Telling those stories isn't always easy. Memory has its own rhythm, and some chapters carry more weight than others. But Marla earned my trust early on. She asked the right questions, knew when to push, and knew when to let a moment breathe. This book exists because she honored my voice—and because she cared about getting it right.

Keeping the Beat is not about reliving the past for nostalgia's sake. It's about passing something forward. If these stories help a young musician, a student, or anyone finding their way understand that discipline, humility, and listening still matter, then this book has done its job.

I'm grateful for the journey, for the music, and for the chance to tell my story in a way that feels true.

Dennis Rowland
Phoenix, Arizona

Preface

As Dennis's collaborator and listener, I want to step back for a moment and explain how this book came to be—and how to read what follows.

So it began, not as a theory, but as a conversation.

What began as a series of informal conversations gradually revealed a deeper pattern. As Dennis reflected on his years with Count Basie—and later revisited Basie's autobiography, *Good Morning Blues*, he began to recognize something he had lived inside of long before he could name it: a set of values consistently modeled, practiced, and sustained across decades of music-making.

Basie never called them principles. He didn't number them or frame them as lessons. But they were there—quietly governing how he led, how he listened, how he kept his band together, and how he treated musicians as both artists and family. Over time, Dennis came to understand these values as a kind of internal metronome—what he would later come to call *Keeping the Beat* ... holding time for others, honoring individuality within collective purpose, and sustaining excellence through trust, discipline, and care.

This book is organized around eight of those observed principles—not as doctrine, but as lived experience. The stories that follow are not meant to mythologize the past, but to illuminate how mentorship works when it is practiced day after day, city after city, bandstand after bandstand. They also invite a broader question that runs quietly beneath the narrative. Throughout these pages, *place* emerges not as background, but as an active force—shaping discipline, expectation, and possibility. In the case of both Detroit and Count Basie's musical world, the answer appears not only in history, but in human bonds that endure.

What you hold here is not simply a memoir, nor a leadership manual, but a reflection on how music teaches us to live together—and how the beat, once learned, stays with you for life.

Dennis says it best: "Only later did I understand that what Count Basie was really teaching me had less to do with notes on a page than with how to live inside music—and inside community.

Long before I could name it, he was showing me what it meant to *keep the beat*: to hold time for others, to listen more than you speak, to trust the people around you, and to create something larger than yourself without losing who you are.

This book is my attempt to make sense of those lessons—to explore what Basie taught me about music, mentorship, and leadership, and how the places that shaped us both helped make that learning possible."

Foreword: Detroit's Jazz Legacy

*"We cannot escape our origins, however hard we try,
those origins which contain the key—could we but find it—
to all that we later become."[1]*
—From James Baldwin's Essay
Many Thousands Gone

If it hadn't been for the time and place of my birth, and my love of jazz and its undeniable role in our country's history, my career as a jazz performer and educator would have been highly unlikely. My life experience is also a fair balance of nature *and* nurture.

Growing up in Detroit in the 1950s and '60s was like being planted in the richest soil any young musician could hope for. I was part of a system—really, a family—that raised musicians the way other towns raised factory workers. Only in our case, the assembly line produced trumpet players, pianists, drummers, singers, arrangers—you name it. Detroit made jazz people.

There's a renown Detroit-born pianist and composer named Kenn Cox who used to play around town late in his life.[2] He was known to say, "The history of jazz and the history of jazz from Detroit are indivisible. You can't tell one story without the other." I couldn't agree more.

---

1   James Baldwin, *Collected Essays*, ed. Toni Morrison (New York: Library of America, 1998), 21.
2   Mark Stryker, *Jazz from Detroit* (Ann Arbor: University of Michigan Press, 2019), xiii

Now, if you ask most folks about Detroit music, they'll say Motown. And fair enough—Motown changed the world. But like Kenn Cox pointed out, Detroit's contribution to jazz is still a secret to many. Detroit has given the world vibraphonist Milt Jackson, guitarist Kenny Burrell, trumpeter Donald Byrd, tenor saxophonists Yusef Lateef and Joe Henderson—and that's just the start. Jazz wouldn't be the same without Detroit.

Mark Stryker, the journalist and author of *Jazz from Detroit*, captures the city's influence. "Detroit has been indispensable to the history of modern and contemporary jazz from the mid-20th century until the present day."[3] He explains that from about 1955 to 1965, during the hard-bop era, Detroit's impact outpaced even Chicago and Philadelphia. If you picked up a jazz record from the East Coast back then, chances were you'd hear three or four Motor City musicians on it.

I came up through Detroit's famous public school music program—one of the best in the country. Back in my day, the city's schools had integrated bands and orchestras, great teachers, and enough funding to put an instrument in your hands and music in your head. We were "part of the primary feeders of talent that sent graduating musicians"[4] in wave after wave to the national stage.

And then there was the mentorship. Barry Harris was the godfather to so many Detroit musicians in the '40s and '50s. He trained players who went on to change the sound of jazz, and because the work was good in Detroit, conventional opinion has it, he stayed longer than a guy with his talent normally might. That meant more of us got the benefit of his teaching and his example.

---

3 Stryker, *Jazz from Detroit*, x
4 Ibid., x

Stryker tells more, "the 1960s and '70s brought tough times—racial strife, civil unrest, economic decline—but the music kept going. Musician-led cooperatives like the Detroit Artists Workshop, Strata Corporation, and Tribe kept the scene alive."[5] Trumpeter Marcus Belgrave became the city's most important teacher for the next four decades, mentoring talents like Geri Allen, Kenny Garrett, Robert Hurst, Regina Carter, and Gerald Cleaver.

Even in the 1980s and after, as the auto industry took hit after hit, Detroit's jazz spirit didn't fade. "It kept punching above its weight class." [6]

The culture of mentorship, the loyal audiences, and the shared musical values kept the fire burning. Stryker says it's a common lineage—partnerships forged in Detroit carried over to bandstands and studios around the world. This was, and still is, the contributing theme of my life in jazz.

I totally agree with his insightful and experienced historical observation, "Detroit musicians are rooted in the bebop tradition—loyal to swing and blues, with a balance of head and heart in their improvisations."[7] That's us. We marry fluid technique with soulful expression. And while we've got players in every style—post-bop, fusion, even the avant-garde—we've always prized fundamentals, individuality, and versatility.

Looking back, I realize how lucky I was to be a kid in Detroit when I was. It wasn't just a city—it was a conservatory disguised as a public school system, a proving ground hidden inside nightclubs and church basements. If you were willing to work, there was always someone ready to teach you the next chord, the next tune, the next truth about

---

5   Ibid., xi
6   Ibid., x
7   Ibid., xii

the music. That's the Detroit I grew up in, and it certainly mentored and grounded me to become the musician and educator I am.

Prologue: Do Places Make People?

Count Basie and his vocalist, Joe Williams, were my Batman and Robin when I was a kid growing up in Detroit in a two-story family flat on Maybury G Street during the 1950s. If places make people, there is a strong argument for that theme in my life. To my mind, Detroit, like a surrogate parent, had an outsized role in my musical education, ability and trajectory in jazz.

Far from beginner's luck or overnight sensation, my journey into the performing arts began when my mama set me on her lap and put my tiny fingers on the keys that made such glorious sounds.   Mama was a sensation herself as a pianist. She was a sought-after accompanist in the church and recital circuit—and her keen ear could spot vocal talent instantly. I was fortunate to hear her trained-ear appraisements, her critiques and helpful tips just through sheer osmosis.

From those toddler days of banging on pots and pans at her feet in the kitchen, and playing with toy instruments and play-acting, our home was like a music and theatre incubator. The comfort of the beat and bop enveloped me like a mama's womb. While she cooked or cleaned up, the kitchen radio might've had some Black Bottom Stomp, big band be-bop, or the swing and stride sounds on the high-fi.

Mom would get the biggest smile and laugh sweetly as we'd go through some of the family photo albums in later years. "I loved dressing you in those cute outfits and taking you on the city Christmas circuit concerts." When I was about kindergarten age, as she told it, she'd slick back my hair, find the matching plaid bow ties with suspenders and she'd be my accompanist on her local holiday ensemble tour: two songs, *How Much is that Doggie in the Window* and *Why Do Fools Fall In Love* by Frankie Lymon and the Teenagers—she said her "little guy" always melted the crowd.

Later, in grade school and junior high, the television variety shows like Ray Anthony and Ed Sullivan, featuring the well-known radio showmen and women of the time, were must-watches in our home. Their pictures on album covers seemed like family surrounding me —breathing vibrancy and musicality into our home—like holograms lifting us into a different sphere.

I didn't want to be anywhere else during those formative years. (Except maybe bouncing the ball on the church playground just next door.) Music and basketball were the two ways a Detroit kid of the 1950s could potentially break free of tenement life, own their own home and, in the motor city where Ford was the dominant employer, aspire to become an independent family man.

My dreams certainly had that solid aspiration and assumption of stability woven in, but I also dreamed of the microphone and singing with a big band as far back as grade school. So, that is how Count Basie, or the 'Chief', as sidemen and the industry knew him, along with Joe Williams, took up residency in the wiring of my brain. Coupled with familial influence, they were two early and significant influences long before I had a conscious, intentional strategy for achieving those dreams.

Now that I'm on the perch of my golden years, I have begun to see how these unique puzzle pieces fit together during those foundational decades. This personal adventure, formed early, allowed me to perform and learn from some of the world's greatest stars. And now, with memories that have become like precious, storied jewels in a family vault, I feel the swift winds of time at my back and an urgency to share these gems.

Having recovered from a stroke in 2012, I certainly recognize my fortune is living to tell about the enchantment of an era—but it is also to share observations that will benefit others. Something more substantial than just a personal collection of memories on paper. I told myself, when Marla asked if I were interested, "If I go to the effort to do this, I need to strive for a helpful, life-lessons collection with Basie as the backdrop."

From the lens of inquiry in this process, what I learned from Basie was exceptional, especially in retrospect. That is why this effort is less a memoir of personal stories and rather a quasi-manual that recounts eight critical principles I saw the Count practice when I was with his new testament band.

Today, as a music instructor at the collegiate level I see myself as a coach who works hard to convey to students these lessons learned—from technique to presence, to etiquette and protocol. This tact has been my focus for the past twenty years.

Coincidentally, I am reminded that Count Basie worked on his autobiography with acclaimed author, musician and historian, Albert Murray, during the last seven years of Basie's life— those were the years I was with him, and the years when I felt like I was his second son —with Joe Williams having been his first son.

These are the strains that burn within my heart in honoring Basie and Joe, and also the legions of peers and performers who poured into me. All of them gave from a deep knowledge base and well-spring within their souls. They taught me how to translate music into a universal language of love and hope.

A Literary Duet in the Making

So, the prompting and excavation began. Marla, who is a student of leadership, began with questions that concentrated on my years with Basie—but she knew we had to build the back-story.

She said, "It interests people to learn what sets mavericks and pioneers apart, like Basie and you. People want to know what went into the making of both of you. Not only the 'who' but the environment, the 'how' and the 'why' you became the humans you were and are. That's why we read biographies and autobiographies. We want the scenery: lessons, conditions, the times, values, teachers and mentors—everything that helped create who you became."

~~~

In the beginning, it was tough recalling some things but with the exercise, clouds began to lift. It became easier to recall, and words came more fluidly the more I plumbed the depths.

Like all duets, they are based on melodies and supporting harmonies. This literary duet has been a process of recollecting timelines and stories based on what happened in the world according to chronicled events. I had not realized, at the outset, how much research would be involved as we tried to verify and build accuracy from some infrequently visited memories. But we did our level best and were committed to mining the Count's autobiography—as well as many books and documentaries on jazz history, Detroit's place in the jazz story and the gifted people who solidified it.

When Surreal Became Real

Some of my earliest memories play like an endless loop—one that never wears out.

Curtains breathing in a summer breeze. A living room scattered with album jackets like a private shrine: Basie. Ellington.
~~~

Goodman. Sammy. Nat. Joe Williams. Jimmy Rushing. Ella. Nancy. Tony. Frank.

I'd be on the floor, propped beside the hi-fi, playing radio disc jockey to an audience of ghosts and giants. Stack the records. Drop the needle. Listen all the way to the last groove. Then— one more time. Always one more time.

You could only load six LPs before the turntable started wobbling like a Frisbee, so you learned patience. You eased the volume up slowly, held your tongue just right, hoping to get away with it before my mother hollered up the stairwell to *turn that thing down!*

Truth is, she loved the music too. So did my dad and my grandparents. Big band. Bebop. Swing. They were jitterbug people— dance people. Music lived in our house the way conversation did.

What I couldn't possibly know then was that years later, the faces on those album covers—the ones scattered around me on the carpet—would step out of cardboard and into my real life. That I'd find myself asking, more than once, *Has this really happened to me?*

I also didn't know that the years I would spend with Basie— those fabled new testament years—would be the final seven years of his life. Knowing that now gives everything more weight. More meaning. It's why the lessons endure.

Threaded through all of it was family.

Bill Basie believed in meals. In conversation. In laughter that came easy and stayed late. He understood that a band wasn't just a collection of musicians—it was a traveling village.

And whenever we were in Detroit to rehearse or record, he encouraged us to invite our families to come be part of it.

The first time that happened for me is burned into memory.

When the bus pulled up to the rehearsal space and my family, along with other relatives of band members, watched us arrive, I felt like I was part of a championship team coming home to a ticker-tape parade. Not applause exactly—something warmer. Something proud.

And in true Southern fashion, my mother didn't arrive empty-handed.

She came bearing down-home love: fried chicken, collard greens, and all the trimmings—home cooking laid out like an offering. Other band members who were local brought their families too, and suddenly the rehearsal room felt less like a workplace and more like a reunion.

I remember bouncing our little daughter on my knee during those afternoons, music in the air, laughter echoing off the walls. And sometimes—because this was Basie's world, Ella would stop by. She always made a point of visiting Basie when she was in town recording. She'd come in, say hello, exchange a few words, bestowing a smile that lit up the room.

For the families, ours and theirs, it meant everything.

Those moments blurred the line between legend and life. Between the records on the floor of my childhood and the people standing right in front of me. The surreal didn't announce itself. It didn't knock.

It simply sat down at the table, passed the chicken, and stayed awhile.

Family, Faith, and Formation

There are so many memories I'm grateful for and it all seemed to start with a dream, an imagination. I am proof that dreams can become reality and what we do as creators of our lives is to bring the unseen into the seen. That is the nature of music and art. A vision, internally so potent, that it begins to out-picture itself for you.

That's what happened to me—but it was not done single handedly. It was supported by everyone around me during my formative years and sometimes, despite my youthful cockiness, my parents, mentors and teachers were able to see the long game better than I.

As I approached my teen years and was starting to notice girls, (piano and voice lessons were well underway, choir and en- semble group gigs were going on and there was a lot of church league basketball competition,) I remember my dad playfully asking me, "Do you want to be like Nat?" My answer was "No, I want to be like Sammy."

Mind you, he knew he was talking to his dreamy-eyed son and correctly considered the inexperienced source. Who knew where or how I would end up, but aspects of people and their talents can be bundled into who we choose to become. Perhaps I created an amalgamation—spirited from those vinyls in the living room long ago.

Surrounded with a solid church-going life at Ebenezer A.M.E. and an education based on music and athletics, there was always someone reminding me that I needed to practice before I went out to play. My loving little grandma would endure my stumbling piano scales—calling out, (God bless her,) "Dennis! Do that over again. That doesn't sound quite right. Check your fingering!" This from a grandmother whose ears were tuned to my mother's capable hands and the use of two pianos in the house. Grandma knew what sounded right—serving as my mother's proxy during those after-school hours when mama was still at work.

The fact that music was the engine of the home was not obvi- ous to me then, but it certainly is now as I reflect on how they supported me. Those loving wings around me, the big band sound (and basketball) were atmospheric—I could not escape those influences if I had wanted to.

My parents and grandparents gifted me with what they knew well themselves: they played league baseball, basketball, softball, track and my mother was a talented singer, pianist and accompanist. Looking back, she had an instinct of creating opportunities for me in my youth, plus having a network of musicians herself, I seemed to be in the right places at the right times. I credit her for bringing Detroit's talented and dedicated teachers into my life who guided me well into my career—one being the great Celeste Cole[8].

It was my mother's doing, I'm sure of it, because she also sang, too, and she knew people—teachers, choir folks, and church musicians. They all seemed to know Celeste or at least know *of* her. Detroit musicians spoke her name with a kind of respect you don't forget. She was a concert singer, an opera artist who had sung all over the world. She had a network so wide you couldn't see the edges of it—teachers, performers, vocal coaches, choir directors. It seemed they all came through her studio.

So when my mother said, "I think you're ready for more." I didn't understand what she meant until I walked into Celeste's studio for the first time. I was around fourteen or so. My voice was still high (and didn't change until my high school years.) I didn't know what fame and accomplishment Miss Cole had but I sure figured it out fast. There she was sitting with me at the piano—this international artist I didn't want to let down. I noticed that the "students" who were coming and going from her studio were all adults—already teaching in Detroit's ju-

---

8 Celeste G. Cole (1926–2013) was an American concert and opera singer who performed internationally before becoming a highly respected Detroit-based vocal instructor. Many of her students were professional vocalists and music educators across Michigan. Dennis was one of her youngest students, a significant early influence on his musical development. See "Celeste G. Cole," *Find A Grave,* https://www.findagrave.com/memorial/217999598/celeste_g-cole.

nior highs and high schools. I had known them through the local concert and recital circuit and stretched my neck bigtime looking up at them. They were always in the newspaper, giving recitals and as far as I was concerned, basically they were center of the universe. These were grown, established people. And then there was me, the young 'un.

But Celeste never looked at me like I was too young. She listened to me sing, sat back, nodded once, and said to my mother on the first visit, "I'll be happy to work with him." And that was it. That was the beginning.

Her studio was something else. I used to sit there waiting for my lesson time and listened to the preceding student—they would always say hello to me as they left, ask how I was doing and acquaintances were made at my ripe age of fourteen. I was in some tall cotton: noticing professionals I knew of, people who had already built real careers—working on their voices and pieces with *the* Celeste Cole. They were good. I mean *really* good. And I was the baby of the bunch. Celeste taught all of them, but somehow, she made room for me, too. I was eating humble pie all the time but diggin' the ear candy and watching these pros doing a vocal work-out like they were in Cole's gym.

From the very beginning, especially after seeing some of these elite musicians work so hard at their craft with Miss Cole, I realized how lucky I was to be in that room. I was surrounded by people who knew more than I did, who had lived more, who had been on stages I didn't even know existed yet. Some of them organized the school and music district choir events and I'd see them running the show—they'd wave at me like we were long-lost colleagues. "Hi Dennis, how are you?" They treated me like I belonged in any setting long before I ever believed it myself.

I didn't understand it then, but what Celeste Cole gave me

wasn't just vocal training. She also gave me access. In sports, we'd call it "playing up". She integrated me into her network that I would draw on again and again when I started performing professionally.

She showed me how to walk into a room full of people who had been doing this a lot longer than I had—and hold my own with the appropriate humility given the age difference. Sure, she taught me about breath and placement, but she also taught me how to listen, discern, how to watch, how to carry myself. In today's parlance, "how to read the room."

"You don't have to be older to belong," she told me once. "You have to be well prepared."

After high school and well into my college years—when I was home on breaks—I'd always arrange to have lessons with Celeste. She shaped the way I understood singing and performing ever before I stepped onto the stages that would define my career.

Looking back, I didn't fully appreciate what a gift it was to be the youngest person in that room. Celeste saw something in me long before I ever saw it in myself. She opened doors that led to almost everything that came after.

Now, when I'm working with my own students, young singers finding their breath, their courage, their sound—I hear her voice in my head. I feel myself reaching for the same patience, the same clarity, the same belief she extended to me without hesitation.

I try with everything in me to pour into them what she once poured into me.

And every time I do, I'm reminded of just how grateful I am. After high school and well into my college years, when I was home on breaks, I'd always arrange to have lessons with my mentor, Celeste Cole.

Why Basie? Why Now?

Knowing a bit about Basie's background, and how he is remembered today, is helpful for framing a view of his leadership, mentoring and influence. Basie was an enigma; not given much to wax on about his life. Writers implored him to do an autobiography long before he began one in earnest with Albert Murray, the renowned music critic, writer and Basie biographer. Theirs spanned seven years of effort—the years I was with him.

Music historians, like many others, have examined the qualities that allowed Basie to lead two of the most highly regarded bands in jazz history, termed the "old and new testament" bands.

I hope to scratch the surface and reveal to you what I saw and encountered during my years with the new testament band. But before we get there, let's briefly delve into who Basie was as the world mourned him at this death in 1984. I'll also share what both music and jazz historians have had to say about his presence on the planet. How they believe Basie masterfully assembled the best talent in the industry through fifty years of changing times that saw World War II, the Vietnam War, the Civil Rights era and desegregation.

He and his bands were affected by it all and that period built the old testament years, as they are referenced in musicology today. The values he built and practiced are what I believe helped establish and create his leadership principles enabling a new testament band to be Grammy award winning in his last decade.

Of course there is this: Basie biographer, Murray, raises the question of "what was Basie's secret as a leader of two of the greatest bands in jazz history— the old and new testament ones?

Murray insight, "As it emerges from (Basie's) his own story, there is the key element of the band as an extension of family life—of a very special kind of togetherness." [9] Thad Jones, speaking with Royal W. Stokes, put it well: *There was a roundness and a togetherness about everything we did that was very exceptional... coming from that strong and binding family circle. It was incredible that a man could organize people to form this strong bond of friendship and generate such a warm, human feeling toward one another, concern for each other's welfare, and consistently maintain it, as Mr. Basie did. That's true genius.* [10]

To this day, I remember that bond. I feel it every time we as performers, past students and now band leaders (and alumni) find one another in the dressing rooms, hotels, venue lobbies and after parties. I don't need to try to apply those principles when I see the gang, it just there. We're family. Inherent because of the love of jazz and the respect we have in knowing that we created a history for today's generation to build upon.

The Final Encore in Harlem

Basie drummer, Gregg Field, and I were trapped in taxi traffic and the decision for me to bail out had to be made. The rain was an on-again-off-again drizzle and the sea of black umbrellas leading up to Abyssinian Baptist Church in Harlem seemed endless. The umbrellas touched and crowded like drenched black-trumpet mushrooms leading up to the steps. Our cab driver knew he was not going to be able to get us anywhere near the front of the church.

Running out of time coming from the hotel, I had miscalculated the rain's impact, and the crowd and the traffic tangle. I needed to be in the choir loft in less than 30 minutes. Sweat dripping

---

9 Count Basie and Albert Murray, *Good Morning Blues: The Autobiography of Count Basie* (New York: Random House, 1985), xx.
10 Ibid., x

down my back, we agreed that Gregg would stay and pay the cab, and I'd bail to run the rest of the way. I just had to keep my eye on those steps and sprint—it was gonna be tight.

I jumped out, picked my way up the curb and through the puddles, frantically weaving my way through the umbrellas. Shouting politely as I could, "Excuse me excuse me excuse me!" The black umbrella sea would part as I pressed, zig-zagging past hundreds as they stood shoulder-to-shoulder lining the street. Finally, getting to the steps and navigating through those who would find standing-room-only spots remaining, I entered through the front door where organ music wafted. I started breathing again and out of my periphery could tell what awaited. Grand old hymns were flowing from the pipe organ. My heart caught in my throat but I had to put my feelings aside and get to the rim, you know what I'm sayin'?

Abyssinian Baptist Church's gorgeous Gothic sanctuary was overflowing—long before the coffin was brought in and mourners had packed the pews.

In news reports it was written that even under umbrellas and in wet coats, those outside refused to leave—suspended in a moment between grief and tribute.[11] It was a day to remember as if a head-of-state was being laid to rest.

Inside the church, music legends were gathered. These were people I had had the fortune to perform with, through the new testament years with Basie, and who were like family to him: Dizzy Gillespie, Cab Calloway, Billy Taylor, Quincy Jones, Sarah Vaughan, Woody Herman, and Betty Carter. I saw them become, in my mind that day, legendary emissaries. No longer as spectators and my friends—but now they were the keepers of the flame— of the jazz legacy Basie had built.[12]

---

11 Tom Miller, "The Abyssinian Baptist Church – 132 West 138th Street," *Daytonian in Manhattan*, November 30, 2022, https://daytoninmanhattan.blogspot.com/2022/11/the-abyssinian-baptist-church-132-west.html.
12 *Ibid.*

This prevailing feeling of mourning and homage was evident, yet when the service began, the energy shifted into one of celebration. As pallbearers emerged carrying Basie's casket down the aisle of the church—where black leaders Adam Clayton Powell Sr. and Jr. had preached—we soloists sang and passages were read.

Basie vocalists, Joe Williams and Carmen Bradford, soloed alongside me like a brother and sister. I sang *It is Right With My Soul*—the organist and I jazzed it up a bit. Often, Basie said, he thought of Joe as his first son, and me, his second son. Certainly, Carmen had to feel she was also close, like family, too. The day forever etched in our hearts.

I was told later that the crowd, standing outside the church, stood silently in the rain through the entire service. One writer recounted, "It was as if they held a collective breath for that last Basie note—an extended 'one mo' time' of farewell."[13] I still get moist eyes when I think about the worshiping public's farewell and the deep emotions of that day.

Step into the Jazz: Who Count Basie Was

From those moments of farewell, you sense that the man being honored was more than a musician—he was a force of musical history throughout the globe beloved for his musicality and band leadership. So, before I share what it meant for me to sing with his new testament band, here's a quick recap of who he was and how the world came to recognize him as Count Basie.

William "Count" Basie was born on August 21, 1904, in Red Bank, New Jersey. From his earliest recollections he said in his autobiography, "One thing I always wanted to do even before I even really thought about being a musician, was to go on the road touring everywhere in the world of show business with a troupe."[14] To know he had these dreams early in life says a lot

______

13 *Ibid.*
14 Basie and Murray, *Good Morning Blues*, 28.

about how he wanted to shape his future.

Ironically, there was an accordion player he says he liked to hear who would play outside a tent every afternoon, and one day he brought the gent a piece of cake from his mother's kitchen. More music and some sage advice flowed when Basie confided that he didn't like school much and would have "rather gone off with a show."[15]

Basie recounts the advice: He told me, "I ought to stick in school and when I finished there would be plenty of time to think about joining a circus or minstrel or vaudeville or something like that. It was very good advice, but the truth is that I would have gone along just to be a water boy for the elephants if I could have. School, I'm sorry to say, was not my thing. I didn't really see any point in finishing school and all that jive. I was only interested in music and show business and traveling.

"That was the whole thing as far as I was concerned, that that was the worst mistake I ever made. I didn't see any connection between geography and history and things like that with traveling. I should have gone on and finished school just like that accordion player with that circus told me to do, but I just wanted to hurry up and get out of there and out of Red Bank and be going somewhere. So I didn't go any higher than junior high school."[16]

After dropping out of school in junior high, he left Red Bank with his best friend, Elmer Williams saying, "We actually left school to go out and make it as musicians."[17] and being the vagabonds longing for Harlem, they shacked up with an Uncle learning the rules and ropes in Harlem. Back in New Jersey, he had attempted to follow in competing drummer Sonny Greer's footsteps, who also lived in Red Bank, but switched to piano after discovering Fats Waller playing organ in Harlem. Waller

---

15 *Ibid.,* 29.
16 Ibid.
17 Ibid

taught him directly, launching Basie's pursuit of the keys.

Eventually he gained jobs playing for well-known vaudeville and burlesque acts and became wide-eyed when listening to Walter Page's Blue Devils on the road one night. He met the band members in time and got a job playing with them, then rinse and repeat happened: another "I've got to be in that band" after hearing them play. It was Bennie Moten's Orchestra and Bennie was a pianist. Basie figured it out, gets the role, Bennie moves into more leadership roles with the band and Basie played. As a commonwealth band, (bands during that time would vote on matters if it affected everyone) they were not happy with the geographical direction and changes that Moten wanted to pursue.

One evening after a show, they voted Moten out and Basie in. Basie said this was the one of the hardest times of his career (the vote, and his vote in particular, because he had never thought he'd be faced with such a thing) and then having to let Moten know of the decision informing him that he, Basie, had been voted in as their new leader.

When the band voted Moten out, Basie took over for several months, calling the group Count Basie and his Cherry Blossoms. When this band folded, he rejoined Moten with a newly re-organized band and played with them until Moten died in 1935 from a failed tonsillectomy.

Thereafter, the band failed to stay together, leading to Basie forming his own nine-piece band, the Barons of Rhythm, with many former Moten members including Walter Page (bass), Freddie Green (guitar), Jo Jones (drums), Lester Young (tenor saxophone) and Jimmy Rushing (vocals).

With the passage of time and the growing interest in swing music now brought into the country's homes via live radio hook-up, the encouragement from the renowned record producer, John Hammond, was critical. Hammond, a civil rights activist and storied music critic helped book engagements expanding to Chicago's Grand Terrace and New York's Roseland Ballroom. The band's Kansas City style—a spontaneous blend of head arrangements and a deep, blues-based sensibility—became the hallmark of their sound.[18]

Basie's famous residency at 52nd Street's Famous Door was a lightning strike: with a bet that if airconditioning were installed coupled with the live radio broadcasts, things could take off, it happened. It was from there when hits like "One O'Clock Jump," "Jumpin' at the Woodside," and "Swingin' the Blues" became national phenomena.

~~~

The "old testament" band (1930s–'40s) continued to feature legends Lester Young, Herschel Evans, Buck Clayton, Jo Jones, and Jimmy Rushing. It was loose, riffbased, blues-infused swing that made the band a jazz standard bearer.

After scaling back briefly in 1950, Basie reformed in 1952 into what became known as the new testament band. This ensemble prized tight orchestration, advanced arrangements by Neal Hefti, Frank Foster, Ernie Wilkins, and Frank Wess, and a modern polish built on Basie's trademark groove.

A national institution then, the orchestra played at John F. Kennedy's inaugural ball, and in 1981 Basie received the Kennedy Center Honor. At that reception, President Ronald Reagan proclaimed Basie was "among the handful of musicians that helped change the path of American music in the '30s and '40s," saying he had "revolutionized jazz".[19]

Even as Basie's health declined after a heart attack in 1976, he

---

18 *Kansas City Blues History*, BluesKC.org, accessed August 15, 2025, https://blueskc.org/kc-blues-history/

19 John S. Wilson, "Count Basie, 79, Band Leader and Master of Swing, Dead," *New York Times*, April 27, 1984, https://www.nytimes.com/1984/04/27/arts/count-basie-79-band-leader-and-master-of-swing-dead.htm
~~~

continued performing after recuperating. Our audiences would see him approaching the stage seated in a motorized wheel-chair, then after standing, be aided—by just a few steps—to the piano, where the crowds' deafening applause would greet him opening the show.

That continued for a time, but when further health issues arose, he went on an extended leave to his home in the Bahamas for a couple of years. Basie was admitted to Doctors' Hospital in Hollywood, Florida, where he died of pancreatic cancer on April 26, 1984.

The story from Harlem's Abyssinian Baptist Church memorial in drizzling rain with thousands of bowed heads, to the storied swing stage—from the old testament riffs of the '30s-40s to new testament elegance of the 1980s—Count Basie's continuing theme legacy is leadership, rhythm, and quiet mastery.

Next, I'll share how working with him shaped the performer and teacher I became—and the lessons I continue to pass on to today's generation of singers.

Introduction

If you had told me at my audition with Count Basie in April of 1977 that nearly seven years later I'd be a soloist at his funeral at New York's Abyssinian Baptist Church singing the great hymn *All Is Well With My Soul*, I would have not believed it.

By the time I joined the band in 1977, the Count's health was fading, but his standards were as sharp as ever. My memories of those years are doubly enriched by the bonds I formed with band members who were like my brothers and sisters—all of us honored to travel the gypsy road throughout the world with the Chief. I was twenty-nine years old when I was recruited to join and most of the sidemen already had decades of experience in the Basie band. Some had been the youngsters in the legendary Basie old testament band.

Humbled is an understatement; I was in awe, you know what I'm sayin? This was the big league; what I had strived for as a life ambition. In their presence I saw what I needed to do and they weren't shy about helping me. The Basie guys were team players wanting everyone to be their best for the worldwide fan base. They took me under their wing.

But with the passage of time, the Captain's health began to worry us. There had been times when we would take a break between the tours, allowing him to get an extended rest in his Bahama home with his wife and daughter. When those health-related hiatuses occurred during those years, we would return to our home ports with our own gigs and stay in touch with our road manager. Sure, we all wanted our patriarchal and beloved leader to live forever, and it was hard imagining what would become of us if and when he passed.

In denial, I purposefully wouldn't let my mind wander in that category too much; I needed to count our blessings for the moment and savor each note we played with him which I did. Toward the end though, it was apparent we were keeping our quiet phone-tree vigils, knowing we would get that call one day.

And then the call came. No cell phones, just home answering machines or grapevine phone trees: the manager tracked me down at a gig I was doing, shared the dreaded news and some of the particulars. He told me I had a ticket to New York, to get there post-haste, to plan on soloing and to choose a hymn befitting of the great Basie.

~~~

When Basie passed, we lost not only a leader, but a master at making music a shared joy. For me, he was a daily reminder that leadership isn't about standing in front, it's about keeping the whole band together, literally and figuratively, and letting the collective musical genius and history soar.

I carry that with me still. Every time I step up to the micro-phone, I listen for his stomp, recreate it in my head and am reminded that the Bill Basie of my heart never really left. In hindsight, Basie's genius lay in his ability to keep the beat not only on the bandstand, but within the human relationships that sustained his music across generations.

Here are the eight lessons I learned from Count Basie. Each one is a quote from his autobiography (pages 382-385) which I've fashioned into chapters along with some interesting stories from my decades in jazz and my years with the Basie band.
~~~

1. "Playing music has never really been work for me… You have to do what you can to keep your band together and also make it stand for something."

2. "The main thing for me is the music… The music and people having a good time listening to it."

3. "The main thing about being the Chief is you get to call the tunes… (so) keep your eyes on the fellow at the piano."

4. "You don't let that stop you if that's what you really want to be."

5. "Trying to play music and have a ball."

6. "Don't be discouraged."

7. "You can still be yourself and grow and keep up with the times."

8. "Count my blessings… I've been very lucky."

KEEPING THE BEAT

CHAPTER 1

Leadership as Stewardship, Loyalty, and Shared Purpose

"Playing music has never really been work for me...
You have to do what you can to keep your band together
and also make it stand for something."
— Count Basie

I saw this every night. For Basie, the music came first. But, the business side mattered because it protected the people making the music.[20] He said that through the years, he always fought for top pay for his musicians—not because the money was the point, but because it meant showing deep respect and honor to the professional musicians behind the world-class band. He also knew that keeping a great band together took both art and stewardship—not unlike a winning coach who has to get into the heads of his players and keep them fired up like an invincible family.

The new testamenters, as we were called, felt Basie's influence as a patriarchal figure who was genuinely proud of his band family and wanted to see our success as players both individually and collectively.

---

20 Count Basie and Albert Murray, *Good Morning Blues: The Autobiography of Count Basie* (New York: Random House, 1985), p. 382

I grew up in a family that practiced the same values, respect and structure. My father and grandfathers were family men who were proud of what their ancestors had overcome. The great migration had lured my grandfather and eight of his brethren from Georgia and Mississippi to the promise of Detroit, landing them in Black Bottom[21].

His stories had a proud, continuing theme: these men were strong, God-fearing providers. Their success in the achievement of making lives and homes for themselves could be heard in his voice as he told tales that echoed of permanence, pride and a claim, too, on what Detroit had become by the time I was in the nest.

So, to me, family life, whether it's in music, theatre, sports or in business is the real backstory for a performer in any realm. Belonging is brotherhood and we long to fit-in. In today's world we can achieve this feeling of belonging in a myriad of ways because technology has narrowed the geographical distance gap. (It can separate us, too, but let's not get hung-up in that rhetorical debate here.)

Back in my Basie days of the seventies and early eighties, technology had not advanced much beyond the rabbit-ear television and an answering machine for the home landline—the only kind of phone we knew. We'd hilariously run to "get the phone" or let it go to the answering machine if we wanted to avoid the number on the read-out, and well, you know how that (still) goes.

So, considering we're social animals and like to sway with the music, the need to feel a sense of belonging was innate among the Basie players. Musicians gravitate to one another as people

---

21 *Black Bottom was a historically Black neighborhood on Detroit's east side, known for its vibrant cultural life and later displaced by mid-20th-century urban renewal projects.* For more background, see "Black Bottom," *Rise Up Detroit,* accessed December 3, 2025, https://riseupdetroit.org/chapters/chapter-1/black-bottom/.

who play together, so we build relatability through our music, like a language in and of itself. With the Captain, he made us all feel that we were a solid, winning team. He was always looking out for us and consequently set the culture as caring for one another—especially since we were seldom with our families in our own homes.

Because he knew first-hand, from decades of travel, how it felt to be away from home and longing for contact with those he and we loved, it was important to him to have every member of the band feel they mattered. That they felt respected and cared for. With that kind of team synergy, a lot like what I found on the basketball court with five guys, we found it natural to work at getting along and tolerated differences when they'd come up. Sometimes, like in the home front, you'd let things go to keep the peace; pick your battles so-to-speak.

People often have asked me if I had felt like I was like a second son to Basie, with Joe Williams being his "first son" as Basie would refer to him. There was no doubt: I did feel like he was a father figure to me. Basie was skilled in providing his vision, his advice, mentoring, direction—but was always interested in my personal life, too. His love language was his attention and caring for every band member, not just me of course. He wanted to know how you were doing and was continuously generous in helping us develop as people and as musicians.

Also, there was a deep sense of belonging I carried with me coming out of Kentucky State's Greek system as a Kappa Alpha Psi. I was member number four of the Alpha Upsilon Chapter in its first years after re-chartering at Kentucky State. Our line name was The Soulful Seven and to this day, those guys are my closest friends. Several of us had been close friends in Detroit before joining the fraternity, but belonging to the same fraternity in college gave us unity and direction—especially at a critical time during our first years away from our family homes in Detroit.

I can see now how those first years at Kentucky State shaped me. It was a privilege to get a full scholarship. I studied hard, practiced hard and learned that HBCUs run in your blood — it's not just school, it's legacy. That's why when my Kappa brothers call me today and say, "Motown, you there?" I laugh. That's my nickname. Always has been. (Only time my mama used my whole name was when I was in trouble—middle name and all. Familiar?)

As we bros settled into our first jobs back at home after college, we ended up in close proximity to one another and raised kids together. Like a cousins club, we were in and out of each other's homes like family, because that's what we were—family and cousins in spirit. (Not surprising because my family-of-origin had lived that way too. There had been seven Rowlands in a two-level family flat. My parents, my brother, grandparents, and aunties. All singing in the church choir, all close. It was loud, musical, and full of love.)

Solid family life and growing up in my parent's home allowed me to see and practice good habits and mental discipline—it also taught me presence. As a youngster, there was always someone in the family making sure I practiced before I went out to play or shoot hoops. That's what made the difference early on.

Now I look back and realize this love for music, family, and fraternity has carried me and has humbled me. Belonging to the fraternity, having lifelong friends write, call and come to the Basie shows when we were in their area of the country, (and later on, my own shows) helped keep me connected to the fraternity and grew my network way beyond what I had experienced at Kentucky State.

I was truly overwhelmed when hundreds of guys would organize and come to a performance. I'd see those smiling bros in the audience and during the parties before and after we'd catch-up on the family goings-on. What great reunions we had. We'd party, play some ball, share stories. They'd say "Motown's in town!" And, that meant something very touching to me—always has.

Family, brotherhood and belonging were the emotional foundation and trifecta for me. Fortunately, my father and grandfathers were great role models, as was Bill Basie.

Looking back, I've tried to hold fast to those memories and my people. I am honored and grateful that they have also held on to me.

The Basie Band is a *family* story that spans decades and has left an indelible mark on musical history. Being there for the last seven years of that story and to experience the impact of Basie's personal values, as it related to his maintaining a family-like culture for us, was the highest of honors.

KEEPING THE BEAT

CHAPTER 2

Purpose Before Ego; Serving the Audience and the Moment

"The main thing for me is the music... The music and people having a good time listening to it."
— Count Basie

"A good time!" Those were the watchwords we heard often that were like a rhythmic heartbeat of the essential man. No matter how long the bus ride or how rough the hotel was, the music was the reason we all kept going. It was the purpose for being, and for Basie the audience's joy was proof that we prevailed in delivering. He simplifies it further, "People dancing or just patting their feet."[22]

That feeling still courses through my veins like muscle memory. The anticipation of a performance, for me and for any seasoned band who has been playing together for a time, we know that feeling of pre-show hype. It's a feeling of moment-to-moment joy. It's the excitement—like a big-game matchup. It's an utter blast to see jazz fans ecstatic with what we're creating in the moment. It is as if they, too, are part of that creation. It's the manna we love.

And it unfolds still today on Sunday evenings in downtown

---

22 Basie and Murray, *Good Morning Blues*, p. 382

Phoenix when the stage lights go up at The Nash, a premier jazz club named in honor of drummer Lewis Nash. It was founded to preserve and advance jazz in Arizona with a focus on jazz education. Through the years, The Nash has become both a proving ground and a sanctuary—a place where tradition meets improvisation. Experiential learning is key and The Nash provides the venue and the audience.

Our Sunday night jam sessions offer musicians of all ages and backgrounds a chance to perform with a professional rhythm section. These sessions are a fulfillment of The Nash's founding dream: to create a continuum where voices and instruments clamor and collaborate in a shared language that speaks clearly and joyfully on Sunday evenings.

As a long-time jazz vocalist and a music educator, the night is a cornerstone for me alongside so many of my current and former students, many who have musical careers or who are educators themselves. It's always a reunion of sorts with people drifting in- and out-of-town, sometimes using the venue to meet-up if they're trying to connect with a friend or another performer who is traveling or based in another city.

Many times, there'll be grand surprises in the faces you see: as in seeing someone you performed with decades ago (if you've had that many birthdays, ahem) and the chance to have them up to the stage to scat or do a song. I can't count the number of times that squeals of delight, moist eyes and long hugs have clogged the aisles a The Nash when performers spot brethren they didn't anticipate running into. That's the deeply shared and uplifting community of jazz on full display.

I usually perform one piece at the end of the evening as a kind of finale—and people tell me that it feels like capstone of the night. They say it's the final blessing before we all go out into the world on Monday to chase after our rainbows. I feel humbled by that honor and never imagined such an honor back when I was 29, or 39 or . . . but now, when I'm surrounded with musicians of all ages and walks of life at The Nash, their presence extends way beyond "just the music". The closer feels like a benediction and an opportunity to remind the squad that we are all connected, supportive, present and blessed to know and "play together"—in that cherished moment in time.

Before the final piece, I try to arrive an hour before to say hello, hear my students from the past or present perform and move quietly through the crowd. There are always familiar faces—many of them former students who are there because these nights to them are part performance, part reunion, and part master class. It's a night that is a regular occurrence for some who never miss it.

(What follows is a conversation between Dennis and Marla, captured just days before the Fourth of July, 2025 over sandwiches at Bertha's Café.)

Marla:

Dennis, it's Sunday night. You're about to go on stage at The Nash. What brings you the most joy at that moment of anticipation when you're getting ready to go on stage to close the night?

Dennis:

Well, I don't always want to be the last performer but usually that's the way it works out because of the length of time allotted to the list on the clipboard of folks who've signed in to sing. I'd rather come on earlier sometimes—'cause I might have something in mind, a couple of songs I want to do.

But when it gets down to that last move, and there's not much time left on the clock... I must change it up from what I might have planned depending on what's been played before, which is always an unknown. Like this past Sunday—soon as I walked in, Raul said, "Don't do a long one." So I said, 'Okay.'

We do what fits into the time slot because the place is staffed by great volunteers who need to clean up and get out of there by a certain time, you know what I mean?

Marla:

And every so often you choose *Every Day I have the Blues,* the jazz anthem that is the well known in the trade and made famous by Joe Williams, Count Basie ... and you've also owned it for the duration of your career as a centerpiece for your performances even when you were with Basie (after Joe went out on his own.) You've performed it countless times and are known to have a unique imprint with your styling—right along with Joe, who was one of your mentors. What's it like today when you perform the piece with your students and "your alumni" at The Nash?

Dennis:

It's like a rally cry or a fight song being belted out at a beloved alma mater! It pays homage to the greats—you know what I'm sayin? *Every Day I Have the Blues.* That's often our Sunday closer and has been with me a long time. Many times we bring up other players and singers to join in. Last Sunday night we had about ten people on stage. That hasn't happened in a while. But when it does—that's the beauty of music's multigenerational reach.

Marla:

Those performers—many are your former students from Scottsdale Community College or Phoenix Union, right? Or pros from Detroit where you were schooled and also taught junior high before your recruitment into the Basie Band?

Dennis:

Some are local students, yeah. And some I've known forever from Detroit. But I know the song, and they know the song, and when that happens, it's like a grand old hymn. We are as one—together. I'm like the conductor. Even if Raul is on piano, I'm co-leading too, quietly. I'm a nice conductor; I don't have to say much.

Marla:

I noticed that. You raise your hands in the air near the end. It's like you're putting a cherry on top. The audience goes wild—because it's been joyful with singing and foot-tapping themselves. For you, it seems it's a closing jam that feels like a reunion, a revival, a family affair?

Dennis:

Yeah, it is. You also see the band's family members in the crowd—beaming. Their people are up there singing with me. And yeah, I think about that. It means something. They let me be the elder now. I wasn't sure if I was going to get to that point, but I'm there. And I'm glad I'm still standing.

Marla:

It's more than standing. You're leading. You're still lifting the room.

Dennis:

Maybe so. I think of it as keeping the song going. The music, the tradition—it doesn't stop. And I like hearing others play *Everyday*. That's what I love about it. It's a true blues tune, so you can go anywhere with it, but it still has structure, Like a good life.

Marla:

That song *Everyday* feels like a foreshadowing element in your life story. The name doesn't just evoke a beloved blues tune, but it hints at something more. The importance of practicing habits that build yourself, everyday—which incrementally seemed to shaped the stamina and discipline you still rely on today?

Dennis:

Well, the song title *Everyday*, if interpreted literally, would be a critical component of my success. Doing those daily reps, either in voice, piano, flute, basketball or school homework— helped build an infrastructure for handling the ups and downs that came later in my career."

Marla:

Do tell.

~~~

When I arrived at Kentucky State University on a full music scholarship, I had two very firm beliefs about myself.

First, I could sing. Second—and this one turned out to be negotiable—I thought I could play basketball.

Not star. Not even starter. I was aiming modestly. Second unit. The second team—that's what it's called in college ball. The guys who practiced hard, came in during scrimmages, and were one rolled ankle away from glory. I figured, *That's me. I belong there.*

I was pretty good. Quick. Skinny. Detroit-skinny. I'd grown up playing everywhere—church gyms, schoolyards, places where nobody asked your position. They could see whether you could hoop. I also believed in coaching. I understood what good coaches did for players, and I wanted that guidance for myself.

Then I walked into open practice.
~~~

The first thing I noticed was the size. These guys weren't just tall—they were built, and many of them had just come off football season. Shoulders like furniture. Legs like tree trunks. Meanwhile, I was built like a reed that sang.

Still, I stuck around. There was an unspoken perk: players ate better. More food. That alone bought me a few weeks of optimism. But reality arrived quickly. I wasn't going to make the roster. No shame in it—just math. I hadn't touched a weight in my life, and at that level, that mattered.

So basketball didn't leave my life. It just moved to the margins—open runs, intramurals, late-night games where nobody cared that I was a singer.

Then, junior year, something unexpected happened.

I was selected to join a performance troupe—students from historically Black colleges—traveling to perform choral and orchestral works. Our first major stop was Denver.

Let me say this plainly: if you think you can sing the same way at 5,000 feet that you do at sea level, Denver will disabuse you of that notion in about three phrases.

I remember thinking I could muscle through it. I went around the form maybe three times—*back to four*—and that was it. Breath gone. Empty tank. The altitude didn't care who I thought I was.

But we stayed. Two, maybe three weeks. And something happened quietly: our lungs adapted. Our phrasing changed. We learned to conserve. To breathe smarter, not harder. Without realizing it, we were training.

From Denver, we flew west to perform at University of California, Los Angeles.

Now here's where the story takes a turn.

When we weren't rehearsing or performing, we played basketball. Summer runs. Open gyms. Serious games. And this was the late '60s—1967, 1968—right in the era of UCLA dominance. You didn't have to know names to know greatness, but some names stuck in my mind.

Sidney Wicks, the future Bruin star. There was also Curtis Rowe, who would later become an NBA All-Star at UCLA— and my timeline overlaps loosely—but I knew Henry Bibby was in the mix too. What mattered wasn't the roster sheet—it was the *experience*.

I played with guys so good I had to apologize mid-possession.

Literally.

"I'm sorry," I told one of them once. "I'm in the wrong spot."

He nodded, like, *Yes. Yes you are.*

And yet—we held our own.

Here's the punchline: after Denver, our choir group entered a Job Corps–sponsored summer basketball tournament. Nobody expected anything. We were singers. Music kids. Out-of-towners.

We won.

Didn't even get the trophy—we weren't officially eligible—but we won the whole thing. That altitude training? Those UCLA runs? They had turned us into something we didn't plan to be.

When I went back to Kentucky State, I wasn't on the team— but I was a different player. Better shot. Better defense. Better conditioning. Denver had followed me home.

And basketball followed me everywhere after that—Louisville parks, Detroit gyms, teaching years, after-school runs with guys who had played at Kentucky State, Tennessee State,

Northwestern, Michigan. They'd walk into a gym and hear, "Oh no. He's here." And sometimes, just sometimes, I'd surprise them.

Especially when they forgot I was a lefty.

And then there was St. Cecilia's.[23]

St. Cecilia's wasn't just a church—it was a crucible. Music. Basketball. Community. For decades, the gym attracted Detroit's best—kids who would go on to the NBA, pros home in the summer, legends dropping in quietly. You learned fast there, or you learned painfully.

That gym still lives on as St. Cecilia Gym, a nonprofit space that continues the tradition—part church basement, part proving ground. You got your ego adjusted there. But you also got better.

Here's the real ending, though—the one I didn't see coming. It changed everything.

Years later, something else crept into my life—almost by accident.

I didn't start lifting weights until I was in my forties, during a stretch of performances in Sedona. You sing at night, rehearse when you can—and during the day, you find ways to stay loose. That's when I started going to the fitness center. Nothing fancy. Just enough to feel better, to stay strong.

---

23 St. Cecilia Church and its gymnasium have played a central role in Detroit's Black cultural and athletic life for decades, producing generations of elite basketball talent and continuing today as the nonprofit St. Cecilia Gym. See *Hanford Sentinel*, "Detroit Church with Black Jesus Mural to Close…" ee "Detroit Church with Black Jesus Mural to Close, Though Family Would Like to See It Continue," *Hanford Sentinel*, accessed [1-18-2026], https://hanfordsentinel.com/lifestyles/faith-and-values/detroit-church-with-black-jesus-mural-to-close-though-family-would-like-to-see-it/article_ef730795-c5fd-4fe7-a5fd-8ba11ee5d28d.html

When I got back to Phoenix, I kept it up. It helped with stamina onstage, helped me hold my body the way singing requires. And when I had my stroke years later, those same habits helped me rebuild. Even now, at seventy-eight, I still have decent grip strength—and I don't take that for granted.

Looking back, it's funny. I never made the Kentucky State team. I never thought of Denver as training. UCLA was just a place we happened to land. Weights came late, almost as an afterthought.

But somehow, all of it stayed with me.

Turns out, I was building something everyday long before I understood how much I'd need it.

CHAPTER 3

Leadership Means Calling the Tune and Staying Present

*"The main thing about being the Chief is
you get to call the tunes ... (and <u>you</u> get to keep your eyes
on the Sparrow)—the fellow at the piano."*
— *Count Basie*

I learned quickly what he meant.

A great band can have a dozen stars, but only one person sets the direction. Basie's humor—calling himself "the sparrow"—was his way of reminding us that leadership could be subtle and unpredictable. Using that metaphor, he was saying we had to stay alert. We may have played a tune a thousand times and could almost do it with our eyes closed, but he was adamant that we not get distracted or check out.

He loved keeping us on our toes. If the audience, the room, or the moment inspired him, he might try something new. He was the one steering the ship. We understood that, and we were better musicians—individually and collectively—because of it. Understanding that was the rule of the road. I was always comfortable under his leadership, from my first performance to my last.

I had grown enormously under Bill Basie's wing, but after several years, I began to feel what I can only describe as a quiet seven-year itch. I started asking myself what it might look like to venture out on my own. How could I take that step without burning a bridge—and while still showing, both publicly and privately, my deep respect for the Chief?

I had no experience navigating a career move like that. Nor did I have a seasoned pro in my corner who could help me interpret the changing landscape I thought I saw ahead. My instinct was to explore evolving tastes in music while I still had a long runway in front of me—to cultivate a new generation of listeners whose ears were moving in new directions. That didn't feel like a shared goal with the Basie band. They were rightly comfortable with the trajectory they were on.

So I kept asking myself: Was I ready? Did I have the resolve to jump onto an independent touring train?

My gut kept answering yes.

Now, with decades of perspective behind me, I recognize this phase for what it was: a natural moment of self-assessment in a young performer's life, when the future feels wide open and the urge to test oneself becomes impossible to ignore.

Building a bridge from the Basie years into a solo career wasn't easy. I had limited name recognition as a soloist, largely because I had never hired a publicist or sought out showboat interviews that might suggest I was trying to eclipse Bill Basie in any way. With Basie, it was always a team sport. His was the name in lights. I never tried to self-promote and felt most comfortable as a committed member of the band.

Around that time, the Count Basie Orchestra won the 1981 Grammy Award for Best Jazz Instrumental Performance, Big Band—an honor that recognizes the strength of an ensemble rather than individual soloists. *On the Road*, the album that earned the award, included my vocals on tracks such as Nat Adderley and Oscar Brown Jr.'s *Work Song*, reflecting my active role in the band's sound during that period.

As was common practice in big-band recordings of the era, vocal credits were often collective rather than individually listed. As a result, my name did not appear in the original liner notes, despite my participation. My agent later explained that this omission made it harder to promote me as a Grammy-award-winning artist. Still, we agreed to test the waters quietly: would presenters and producers be interested in a Dennis Rowland tour, especially in places where audiences had already seen me perform with Basie?

As luck would have it, that question was answered sooner than expected.

When the Basie band began a Japanese tour that year, a local producer asked me, "Mr. Dennis, are you on the show's *On the Road* album?"

"Yes, I am," I said.

"Well then," he replied, "how do you spell your name? We need to add you to the liner notes."

That simple exchange turned out to be a turning point. My name was added to the Japanese release of the album—something I didn't even see until years later, when I returned to Japan on my own. I've often thought fate had a hand in it. That recognition became one of the reasons my following there grew so quickly and so deeply.

The kindness I encountered in Japan ran deeper than professionalism. Shortly after the Grammy announcement, while still touring with Basie, we had a few days off in Osaka. Someone approached me and said, "Dennis, would you like to play our club? We'll take care of everything—train ticket, first-class hotel, rehearsals." And they did.

I stepped into that engagement fully supported, well cared for, and warmly received. Looking back, it felt like the universe quietly saying, You'll be all right.

Not long after, my agent called. "Osaka wants you back," he said. "They've mapped out a tour." We didn't hesitate. Over the next several years, I toured internationally and extensively. My agent has never forgotten the first country beyond U.S. borders to reach out wasn't Europe or South America, but Japan. They became the bridge between my Basie years and a solo career that would span decades.

People still ask me where I found my best audiences.

I always answer the same way: Japan.

They welcomed me when I needed it most. It wasn't simply the next chapter of my career—it was a golden stretch. Later, I returned with Ray Anthony. I toured Spain with Frank Foster, who had played with Basie in the 1960s and went on to lead his own band. Each step built on the last.

Looking back now, I'm grateful I listened to that instinct. Stepping out on my own gave me the freedom to explore, to stretch, and to discover what I was capable of beyond the framework I had known so well. Those years confirmed something important: honoring where you came from does not prevent you from answering where you're meant to go.

Basie taught me how to stay present, how to listen, and how to lead without forcing the music. Carrying those lessons forward—and finally listening closely enough to call my own tune—made all the difference.

CHAPTER 4

Resilience, Determination and Staying the Course

"You don't let that stop you if that's what you really want to be."

— Count Basie

"As far as all the traveling and bumping around is concerned… I didn't intend to let anything stop me… Life is a bitch, and if it's not one damn thing it's going to be something else… You don't let that stop you if that's what you really want to be."[24]

Detroit teaches you early that wanting something isn't enough. You have to stay with it. You get knocked around, slowed down, overlooked, or told to wait your turn—and you learn quickly that none of that is a reason to quit. As Basie said, you don't let that stop you if that's what you really want to be. You keep moving. You adjust. You endure.

I grew up in Detroit in the 1960s, when music wasn't just entertainment—it was aspiration. Motown was taking shape in real time, and for those of us coming up inside it, the message was clear: talent mattered, but resilience mattered more. Music

---

24 Basie and Murray, *Good Morning Blues*, p. 382

and basketball were my twin educations. They taught discipline, humility, timing, and how to read a room—skills that carried me everywhere I went.

Detroit musicians didn't come out sounding the same because the city didn't reward imitation. You learned by listening, by sitting in, by getting called out when you weren't ready and welcomed back when you were. Jam sessions were classrooms. Older musicians were professors who didn't lecture—they played. If you couldn't hang, you didn't get coddled. You got better.

That environment produced discernment. Even now, I can hear the difference between a vocalist who grew up at the birth of Motown and someone who arrived ten or twenty years later. It's subtle but unmistakable—the phrasing, the emotional economy, the way a singer sits inside the groove. Those early voices carry the sound of formation, not reproduction. Once you hear it, you can't unhear it.

Detroit rewarded originality. Nobody wanted you to sound like someone else. You were expected to sound like yourself, and you earned that voice through repetition, failure, and persistence. The city shaped artists who understood struggle—not as tragedy, but as process.

And Detroit didn't just produce musicians. It produced strivers.

Which brings me to basketball—and to a night at the Fisher Y on Grand River.

~~~

Wherever I went in the world, I packed two uniforms.

One was the suit for the gig — the one with the good shoes and the tie that didn't wrinkle in the suitcase.
~~~

The other lived in the side pocket of my bag: beat-up sneakers, a pair of shorts, and a T-shirt that already knew the smell of a gym. Because if I had a day off in any city — Vegas, L.A., Honolulu, Madrid—I was going to find a run. A Y, a church league, some city park with bent rims and good players.

Music took me everywhere. Basketball made those places feel like home.

Back in Detroit, before all that travel, my main spot was the Fisher Y over on Grand River. That place was serious. You didn't stroll in there unless you could actually hoop. We had school teachers who could still go, a couple guys who'd played college ball, and a few local legends everybody in the city knew by first name only.

After graduating from Kentucky State, I'd come back to Detroit thinking I could still really play. The Fisher Y guys were happy to let me know where I stood—a leftie with the nickname, Motown. Those guys let everyone know real quick where they stood and no one's head got too big too fast. (There were All Americans from all over in that Y.)

This one night, we're warming up. Just that pre-game rhythm: a couple of us on the wings, somebody working on their handle at the top, a big man down low trying to remember his post moves. Ball bouncing, shoes squeaking, trash talk warming up along with the jump shots.

Door opens. In walks this slim brother in a sweatsuit and a cap pulled down just enough to make you look twice.

Now, in a place like the Fisher Y, you see all kinds: guys getting off work at the plant or the office, college kids home for the summer, old heads who swear they "used to be somebody" and want to come out and prove it. But this dude… he had a different kind of quiet on him. Not shy, just… contained.

One of the fellas gives him the usual Y greeting: "Yo, you runnin'?" He just nods.

You can tell who's a real baller before they even touch the ball. The way they walk onto the court, the way they stretch, the way their eyes scan who's already out there, working out matchups in their head. This brother had that.

Somebody rolled the ball his way. He caught it smooth, like the ball already knew him, took one dribble, rose up, and that jumper… man. Soft. Net didn't even complain.

A couple of guys looked over like, Oh, okay, he's not just here for cardio.

Now, the thing is, I knew exactly who he was.

I'd seen him around Motown. Heard the records, watched him move through a room with that same quiet. He already had hits. This was before *What's Going On*, but believe me—he was not some unknown singer trying to make it. He was already *that* guy.

But there, at the Fisher Y, he was just a tall guard in a cap who could stroke it from mid-range.

So we're picking teams. I end up on his squad, which I was very happy about, thank you. I bring the ball up, he's on the wing. First possession, I drive, defense collapses, kick it out to him. He's wide open.

Now, I got a decision to make. I could say it—"Man, I know who you are"—and watch the whole gym shift. If that happened, suddenly dudes stop playing ball and start playing "impress the star." Or, I could just treat him like any other hooper who came to get some run and some peace.

I went with option two. I just gave him a nod.

"How you doin', bro," I said, like we'd been running together for years, and swung him the ball.

He caught my eye for half a second before he shot. There was a whole conversation in that look: Yeah, you know. Yeah, I know. And yeah, I'm not gonna say anything.

Bucket.

Next trip down, he hit me with a beautiful little no-look pass in the lane. I finished it and now *we* had a thing going. Two musicians talking without words, but in this case the music was pick-and-roll, backdoor cuts, and jumpers from the elbow.

We ran for a couple of games like that. No fuss, no autographs, nobody stopping the run to ask about Motown. Just hoops. Couple of the brothers even started calling him by some made-up nickname, like "Bruce" or something, because they genuinely didn't know who he was.

I knew. And he knew I knew.

When the night wound down, we did what ballers do. Slap of hands, little half-hug. "Good run, man," I said. "Yeah, man," he answered. "Come on back." I said.

That was it. That's how the whole thing started.

Later on, when life moved us both into different rooms — private parties, backstage situations, those little VIP corners where the famous people go to escape the people who are excited to be near famous people—we'd run into each other again.

And every time, there'd be that same little nod: *Fisher Y.* That was the code. And it formed a bond for us.

Not "Hey man, I'm such a big fan," even though I was. Not "Remember when we played at the Y?" with a big loud story in front of everybody. Just a quiet understanding: for at least one night in Detroit, he got to be just a baller, and I helped protect that.

And you know, that thing at the Y wasn't just about him. All over the place, wherever the music took me, I was doing the same thing.

We'd hit a city with the band, or I'd be in town for a show, and if I had a free afternoon I'd find a Y. Back then, you could go to pretty much any Y in the world with your card. Some places let you sleep there cheap. I'd show up, lace 'em up, and suddenly I wasn't the singer from Basie's band or the guy on the poster. I was just Dennis, running the floor, trying to keep some church-league point guard from embarrassing me.

Hollywood Y? Same deal. You'd have actors in there who you'd recognize immediately from TV shows and movies, and the unwritten rule was simple: if they wanted to be "that guy," they'd let you know. If not? They were just another player calling out screens and asking, "Who's got next?"

Hawaii, Japan, Europe or stateside—it was the same language. Ball is universal. A good screen, a clean pass, a hard foul followed by, "You good, man?"—that's diplomacy in sneakers. I played with dudes who later turned up in commercials or in the credits of movies. A couple of cats from the Detroit Lions even ended up singing background on a certain classic record, bringing those Fisher Y pipes into the studio.

The music world and the basketball world overlapped more than people think. Over the years, I realized I had this little role whenever I was around people with more notoriety than I did— the real "household name" folks. On the court, on stage, at a party, I'd watch how they walked in, how they carried themselves, and I'd take my cue from that.

If they wanted to hold court, cool. I'd help manage the energy, keep folks from getting too wild. If they wanted to disappear into the crowd and just *be*, I'd help protect that bubble—change the subject, keep the conversation light, treat them like any other brother grabbing a plate or catching a rebound.

Letting people "be"—just be a baller, just be a musician in the section instead of the star on the poster—that's one of the kindest things you can do for somebody who lives in the spotlight. It's respect. It's trust. It's saying, "I see all that you are, but I also see the human who just wants to run full-court and work up a sweat."

That night at the Fisher Y, I picked up on that from his eyes: *Please don't make this a thing. Let me just hoop.* So I didn't make it a thing. I just played ball with him.

And later on, when the whole world was asking, *"What's Going On,"* I could smile to myself and remember that before all the history and the headlines and the greatest-songs-of-all-time lists, there was just this quiet brother in a cap at the Y on Grand River—knocking down jumpers, blending in with the fellas, happy to be invisible for a couple of games.

Marvin Gaye, ladies and gentlemen.

<div align="center">~~~</div>

What struck me later—long after that night—was how much that moment said about Detroit.

Here was Marvin Gaye, already successful, already known, choosing a gym over a spotlight. Wanting, just for a couple of games, to be nobody special. Detroit made space for that. The city understood that before you are celebrated, you are shaped—and sometimes you need to return to the place that shaped you.

That night at the Fisher Y wasn't about protecting a celebrity.

It was about honoring a shared code. Detroit raised people who knew how to work, how to wait, and how to keep going when the world made it hard.

Marvin didn't ask to be protected. He asked, silently, not to be interrupted. And I understood that instinct because Detroit had taught it to me too.

Later, when the world would ask What's Going On, I already knew part of the answer. What was going on was resilience. Discipline. Staying the course. Not letting the noise stop you from becoming what you were meant to be.

That's Detroit. And that's the lesson Basie was talking about all along.

CHAPTER 5

Joy as Fuel; Fun as a Serious Leadership Principle

"Trying to play music and have a ball."
— ***Count Basie***

Basie didn't dress it up. He didn't overthink it. He didn't moralize it.

If you were going to make music worth listening to, you'd better be enjoying yourself while you did it. Fun wasn't optional, it was structural. Lose the joy and the swing went with it.

That idea sounds simple until you realize how much stood in the way of it. In his autobiography, Basie talks plainly about the Jim Crow realities his band endured during what is called its old testament years—decades before I ever came along. Then, segregation wasn't theoretical. It showed up in hotels, restaurants, travel routes, and backstage doors. Still, Basie refused to let bitterness become the soundtrack.

"I'll just say I was out there trying to do what I was trying to do," he wrote, "which was to play music and have a ball. I wasn't surprised when things got strange one way or another…

I didn't intend to let anything stop me if I could help it.[25]"

That should tell you something.

Before I ever joined the Basie band in 1977, joy had already been threaded into my life—not naïvely, not without struggle, but deliberately. I grew up in Detroit in the long echo of the Great Migration[26], which didn't truly wind down until the 1970s. My family was part of that movement north—people chasing work, safety, dignity, and possibility, carrying culture with them like luggage you don't check at the station.

Postwar Detroit was alive. Gospel poured out of churches. Jazz and big band music spilled from radios, porches, and living room record players. It was a city vibrating with promise and tension at the same time—and for a kid born into a family that sang, danced, played ball, and loved the swing sound, it was fertile ground. Looking back now, I know there was a lot of joy moving through those rooms—among my parents, my aunties, my grandparents. A lot of music. A lot of laughter. A lot of rhythm.

My mother was gifted both musically and athletically—an accompanist in demand, the kind of musician singers relied on. Her people came up from Laurel, Mississippi. My father's family came from Georgia. Like so many others, they arrived in Detroit during the Great Migration and built lives that mixed hard work with community. Further back, ancestry reports trace my roots to Nigeria, the Western Bantu peoples, and Benin and Togo—markers without timestamps, but with resonance.

---

25 Basie and Murray, *Good Morning Blues*, p. 383

26 Wilkerson, The Warmth of Other Suns, p. 9. Wilkerson writes, "Over the course of six decades, some six million Blacks left the land of their forefathers and fanned out across the country for an uncertain existence in every corner of America. The places they went were big, frightening and already crowded—New York, Detroit, Chicago, Los Angeles, Philadelphia and smaller, equally foreign cities—Syracuse, Oakland, Milwaukee, Newark, Gary. Each turned into a 'receiving station and port of refuge,' wrote the poet Carl Sandburg, then a Chicago newspaper reporter documenting the unfolding migration there.

My dad was my model for balance. He loved the saxophone and listened to all the big bands. He loved baseball and softball, too, which meant church leagues, long afternoons, and plenty of socializing. By day, he worked as an accounting clerk; by night, he took on bookkeeping and tax prep clients because he genuinely enjoyed helping people. I helped him sort receipts occasionally—enough to know, early on, that paperwork wasn't going to be my thing.

But music? Music was fun. And fun, I would later learn, was serious business. Basie made it that simple. Fun was essential. If the joy was gone, so was the swing.

~~~

In 1977, and teaching junior high music in the Detroit public school system, Motown had happened, disco was king, punk was rising, and jazz was shifting from dance floors to concert halls. America was in the aftershock of Vietnam and Watergate.

In addition to my teaching job, I had been singing with the Jimmy Wilkins Band in Detroit when I got the call to come for a try-out with Basie. Basie was getting back on the road after a stroke and needed someone for the male vocals. I auditioned during the time of Detroit's summer music festival and Jimmy just happened to be Northwestern's band director. (Jimmy, who had played with Basie years before, along with this renowned saxophonist brother and arranger, Ernie Wilkins[27] had all the arrangements, charts etc. The prep work was really in helping the kids learn the charts.)

So, it came to pass: we rehearsed the gang on *Everyday* and a couple of other tunes I'm pressed to remember, and as you'd

---

27 "Ernie Wilkins was a tenor saxophonist, arranger, and composer closely associated with the Count Basie Orchestra, contributing significantly to its postwar sound. See "Ernie Wilkins," The World of Sax, https://theworldofsax.com/
~~~

expect we were prepared—tight, strong, no nonsense. With the strong foundation of Jimmy and I playing together in his band for years, the audition came off well—but you're still nervous until you actually hear the verdict.

Basie and his right-hand-men, Sonny Cohn and Bill Hughes, had been at the audition and asked me and my dad to meet them afterward at Carl's Chop House. That could be good news (my dad and I said to ourselves,) but still . . .

After the pleasantries and entrée order, Mr. Basie cut right to the chase and said to me and my dad, "Son, we'd like to have you in the band. You're very good. You're not going to get rich—but you're going to get better." And that was it.

I said, with eyes probably bulging out of my head and a kick under the table with my dad, "Yes, sir!"

Looking back decades later, I see my 29-year-old self believing I was hot stuff—but at the first practice, I could see I was in some very tall cotton. That former self-image was abruptly halted. I ate my own humble pie, privately and quietly. Observing these cats and interacting with them? They were serious and I had a lot to learn. Some didn't really give me the time of day for a couple of years; pleasant, yes, but to them, I was a total rookie.

~~~

I always say I owe that audition to two people: Jimmy Wilkins, who let me borrow his entire high-school band to rehearse with—and a tiny, sharp-eyed woman named Midge Ellis[28]. If

---

28 Midge Ellis—"Mama Jazz" to all of us—was the tiny 5'2" powerhouse who held Detroit's whole jazz world together. She looked after young players like we were her own, and she had deep friendships with giants like Basie, Buddy Rich, and Maynard. Folks called her a global jazz consigliere, and they weren't kidding. *Midge Ellis, a Champion of Jazz in Detroit, Dies at 91,"* Jazz Promo Services, January 17, 2015, accessed 12/14/2025, https://jazzpromoservices.com/jazz-
~~~

Jimmy prepared me, Midge is the one who put the wheels in motion.

If you spent enough years playing around Detroit—church gigs, union halls, private clubs, those little supper clubs that felt glamorous only until the lights came up—you eventually ran into Midge Ellis. And once she took an interest in you, she never forgot your name.

Midge wasn't a singer, and she wasn't a musician, not in the way the guys were. She was something harder to define. A connector. A fixer. The person who always knew who was in town, who needed a sub, who had just left a band, who was looking to hire. She worked in jazz promotion for years—Basie's people, Stan Kenton's circle, God knows who else—and she had this uncanny ability to see where someone belonged before they could see it themselves.

By the time she crossed my path, I was already teaching school at Munger Junior High and gigging every night I could. That was just how Detroit musicians survived. You taught during the day, played at night, prayed the check cleared, and hoped the furnace didn't die during the winter. And somehow, even with all that noise, Midge heard me.

She came up after a gig once—not asking for anything, just watching me with this amused little smile that made me wonder if she knew something I didn't. A couple of weeks later, she said, "You ever thought about singing with Basie?" Just like that. As if she were asking whether I'd ever tried the peach cobbler at Flood's.

I laughed it off at first. Guys dreamed about singing with the Count, but nobody said it out loud. It felt superstitious, like saying it might jinx the whole idea. But Midge wasn't joking. She'd been keeping tabs on me—she told me later—hearing

news/midge-ellis-a-champion-of-jazz-in-detroit-dies-at-91-3/

about me from musicians she trusted, seeing me around town, watching me grow into my voice.

She's the one who lined everything up. She knew Basie's schedule, when the band would be in Detroit, who the road managers were, who would actually get things done. Unbeknownst to me, she'd had dinner with Basie and in their usual banter and conversation, told him she thought he needed to hear me. With that she arranged for Sonny Cohn, Bill Hughes and Basie to come to Northwestern High. I didn't ask her until much later how she finagled that—I just knew at the time it had her fingerprints all over it. Nobody else in town could make that kind of magic happen.

And when the audition ended—when the band room door closed, and my father and those Basie men and I were headed to lunch at the Chop House—Midge was not there. She stayed quiet. She wasn't looking for credit. She never did. But I knew she'd hear what the outcome was.

A week or so later, I was onstage somewhere—can't remember the club, just remember it was one of those long nights where the smoke hangs low and the crowd leans in close—and one of the waitresses waved me to the phone.

"This is Midge," she said, no hello, no small talk. "What are you doing next week?"

I told her my gig schedule.

She cut me off. "No. You're going to New York by way of Dayton with Basie."

That was her way of telling me I was "in" even before the official tour to Europe in the new year. Not ceremonious, not dramatic. Just fact.

I didn't have a passport yet, so I couldn't go to Europe with the band that fall. But Basie let me join them on that short run before they left—Indiana, Ohio, Illinois, a quick swing that felt like arriving in another universe. When they came back from Europe, my passport had finally arrived, and I humbly stepped onto that bus as a full member of the Count Basie Orchestra in early1978.

~~~

What I'll never forget during the succeeding years were the "after shows"—Basie guys, old friends from Detroit, jamming till sunrise. People I grew up with in Detroit would show up in cities all over the country. We'd meet after gigs and bring the music home again. It wasn't just a tour. It was a brotherhood. And it shaped me. People talk about getting lucky breaks like they're accidents. But mine wasn't an accident.

It was Midge. She didn't play an instrument. She didn't sing. But I'm telling you—she changed the sound of my entire life.

And once Midge opened that door, the rest moved fast—faster than I ever imagined. One minute I was teaching at Munger, singing with Ernie and his band, hustling gigs at night, and the next I was out on the road with one of the greatest bands in the world, learning more in a month than I had in the ten years before it.

My first two weeks with the band were pinchable moments. You can imagine the joy of hearing back-to-back greats such as Ella Fitzgerald, Sarah Vaughan, Billie Eckstein and Tony Bennett singing with the Basie band. Talk about education. What an honor it was to lead off the first set on Bennett's night with Basie in Belmont, NY, when he offered me his arrangement of *Watch What Happens* to open with. Of course, I've used that coveted arrangement ever since. But on the road with Count Basie, time felt suspended. Night after night, city after city, the band brought swing to life. No Auto-Tune. No
~~~

backing tracks. Just horns, rhythm, and the realization that my voice from Detroit was stepping into the spotlight for a few pieces. Humbling and learning continually.

I saw how much fun the Count himself was having as we energized the audiences, how he honored the effort it took for them to be there, making the audience feel they were part of the production. It was like that: performers know that audiences shape the outcome. Music lifts spirits and the venue becomes its own pulsing heart.

That was the central theme: you go through quite a journey to get to the joy as a performer and when you feel it, it's infectious. Your audience not only shapes it but also feels the emotional sound wave you ride together. Playing music and having a ball—fun indeed.

CHAPTER 6

Patience, Persistence and Building Trust Over Time

"Don't be discouraged."

— Count Basie

Count Basie admitted later that getting into Bennie Moten's band began as a scheme. A careful one. Moten's was the top band in the West, and Basie knew exactly how high he was aiming—even if he didn't yet know how he'd get there.

As I mentioned earlier, Basie was already riding high with the Blue Devils, an achievement earned the hard way through years of burlesque pits, blues singers, and learning how to make music work night after night. But talent alone wasn't enough. Timing mattered. Proximity mattered. Who you knew mattered. And Basie kept circling one impossible question: how does a piano player get into the Moten Band—literally the band of another piano player? What band needed two piano men?

According to his autobiography and historical record, the door finally cracked open through Moten's brother. Once inside, Basie didn't rush anything. He focused instead on bonding with the sidemen—earning trust, showing he could sub seamlessly when Moten stepped away to handle business matters, and proving he understood the band from the inside out. What he didn't anticipate was what came next.

Moten was facing growing tension within the group. He wanted to take the band onto a circuit the musicians opposed, and dissatisfaction spread. As a Commonwealth Band, the ensemble operated collectively—long before unions formalized such structure—meaning decisions that affected the band were put to a vote. When that vote came, it changed everything.

The musicians chose Basie as their next leader.

What followed, according to Basie, was the hardest conversation of his early career. Basie had to tell Moten—the man who had given him his chance—that the band had voted him out as leader. It was ambition and humility colliding head-on, and by all accounts, the transition was handled with respect and grace. Soon after, the band became Count Basie and His Cherry Blossoms.

I tell you this to express, in my opinion, that this was leadership in its most human form: set your sights high, earn your place quietly, and build trust until responsibility finds you.

That kind of patience—the willingness to work a long angle without knowing the outcome—was something I would come to understand firsthand.

Like Basie's burning desire to be in Moten's band, there was a bit of a scheme in my early life, too.

~~~

I never planned on becoming an anthem singer. Not at first, anyway. What I really wanted—what I schemed for—was a way to get myself into Pistons games without bankrupting my
~~~

little teacher's salary. I had grown up breathing Piston's air.

Some people in Detroit inhaled automobile exhaust; I inhaled NBA box scores. My father and I would be on the phone half the week, pacing and arguing about draft picks as if any of it depended on us. When the Pistons got the number two pick in '66, we thought for sure we were getting Cazzie Russell—homegrown Michigan royalty. But the Knicks snagged him first, and Detroit took this kid from Syracuse named Dave Bing.

I remember looking at the television afterward and telling my dad, "Don't worry about it. Bing's gonna be the man." And boy, was he.

By the time we paired Bing with Bob Lanier in 1970, Detroit basketball was getting real again. And I wanted to be in that building—to watch history breathe in real time.

But ticket prices? Out of reach. So I did the only sensible thing:

I angled for singing for my supper. Or rather, sing the National Anthem for a ticket to a Piston's game.

This whole caper started because the Pistons' organist was leaving, and I happened to know someone who could fill that seat—my friend Tyrone Hemphill, a brilliant organist from around town. I told someone who was playing with us from the Pistons' office that I had heard their guy was leaving and said, "Listen, I got your new guy. You'll love him."

Turns out, they did.

And on top of that, Tyrone is the one who got me my anthem audition.

See, during timeouts we'd already been singing holiday tunes, little jazz riffs—just enough to let the arena folks know we had more in our pockets than "Jingle Bells." Tyrone nudged: "You ought'a try out for the anthem, Dennis."

Truthfully?

I wanted the tickets. The prestige was gravy.

Next thing I knew, I'm going through the employee entrance, trying hard not to look like a tourist or trip over my own shoes.

The players' entrance wasn't anything like what stadium or arenas are today. There was one man posted up, Earl B, who greeted you like you were walking into his living room.

"Ohh, Dennis! You singing tonight? Go on in, son, go on in."

Just like that.

Warm Detroit hospitality. Open sesame.

At first, standing on the court, I couldn't see much past the lights. I couldn't tell if anyone important was even watching. I was just trying to stay upright and not knock over the microphone.

But after a few games, once I relaxed into it, I realized who was actually there.

It was Motown. The front office. The press. The players. The legends visiting from out of town.

And the Pontchartrain Hotel—where half the league hung out after games—became my unofficial second workplace. I'd drop in with Jimmy Wilkins' big band, sit in on tunes, and the players invited me to join them like we'd known each other since the playground.

Dave Bing, Bob Lanier, Curtis Perry, Connie Hawkins, Walter Davis—they were all part of that orbit.

And because the anthem gig didn't pay cash, the team kept me swimming in excellent seats, warm meals, and the kind of press-room conversations money couldn't buy.

Every time I walked in, they'd say, "Dennis, you singing tonight? Good luck, man."

What started as a little hustle to get into the arena became an entire ecosystem—friendships, opportunities, musical gigs, and a network that eventually followed me clear across the country.

Looking back, that anthem wasn't just a song. It was a key— one that unlocked rooms or opportunity and life-long friendships I could not have imagined.

~~~

People always assume I met Al McCoy in Phoenix—maybe backstage at the Coliseum, or somewhere in the tunnels where the Suns used to roam. But no. I met him in New Orleans, in a jazz club called Rosie's, of all places.

I was touring with Basie then—into a few years of one-nighters, hotel lobbies, and stages that smelled like wood, whiskey, and history. Rosie's was packed that night, shoulders touching shoulders, the air thick enough to chew. We kicked into one of those Basie sets that seemed to float two inches above the ground.

Mid-song, as I scanned the room, something tugged at my attention. A familiar profile. A coach's posture. A face I'd seen on television broadcasts and in NBA write-ups. Cotton Fitzsimmons.

I nearly broke into a huge laugh right there on stage. What were the odds? The Detroit kid in me was tickled pink recognizing the Phoenix Suns coach across a smoky New Orle-
~~~

ans jazz club. When the set ended, I didn't hesitate. I walked straight to him.

"How you doing, Coach?"

His eyebrows jumped like I'd surprised him in his own living room.

"Well now," he said, laughing, "not many folks pick me out in a jazz crowd."

That's when he gestured to the man beside him.

"Dennis, meet my friend Al McCoy."

Al McCoy—the voice of the Phoenix Suns. The man whose words had narrated decades of basketball lore in the Valley.

I extended my hand and with a sly tone, "I think I know you…"

Al chuckled. "Of course you do."

The three of us talked as if we'd been doing it all our lives: about Basie, about basketball, about the Suns' rhythm and swing.

Before they left, Al leaned in close and said,

"Next time you're in Phoenix, Dennis, let me know. I want you to sing the anthem for us."

That night opened a door that would stay open for decades.

And the story didn't end there.

Just before Al passed away, he came to hear me perform at the Ravenscroft—the stunning jazz venue in Scottsdale known for its perfect acoustics and intimate feel. The room was full that night, but I spotted him easily amid the faces. You couldn't miss that presence, that warmth.

During the show, I paused and called out to him gently, "Al, would you like to come up and sing one with us?"

He smiled—that soft, gracious, broadcaster's smile—and declined in that elegant Al McCoy way, a gesture that somehow carried humility, humor, and a lifetime of gratitude all at once.

But he was there. In the room. Listening. And I will never forget the feeling of singing to him that night. One of the last times I saw him. One of the last times Phoenix's greatest voice sat in an audience instead of above an arena. When he passed, the whole city felt it.

I carry that Ravenscroft night with me—quiet, beautiful, unexpected—just like the night I first met him and Coach Fitzsimmons in a smoky club in New Orleans. His picture adorns the cover of my ever-present notebook of arrangements; I don't go a day without remembering Al.

Sometimes the threads that stitch your life together begin in the most unlikely places. And if you're paying attention—if you spot the right face in the crowd—your whole story can change.

Basie recognized an opening when most people would have talked themselves out of it. So did I. Neither of us knew where it would lead—only that it felt right to step forward. That's the part people miss. The scheme isn't the point. The patience is. The persistence is. And the trust you build along the way is what makes the door worth opening when it finally swings wide.

CHAPTER 7

Adaptability Without Abandoning Identity

"You can still be yourself and grow and keep up with the times."

— Count Basie

"I was always game… if something came up, I was willing to try it. You can still be yourself and grow and keep up with the times."[29]

I took that to heart. Basie didn't reinvent himself every decade—he expanded. He stayed rooted, but never stuck. He didn't chase trends; he stayed curious.

That idea became a guidepost for me. Be who you are—and who you're called to be. If there's a throughline in my life, it's that desire pulls you forward. When you want something badly enough, you find a way to move toward it. To me, that desire feels like something sacred—undeniable divinity at work inside you.

When Basie talked about being "always game," he meant being willing to bet on yourself.

"I mean being willing to take a big chance on yourself because you want to do what you want to do," he said. "I was always

---

29 Basie and Murray, *Good Morning Blues*, p. 384

willing to say, 'Let's see what happens,' when something came up that looked like it might get me a little closer to where I wanted to be."[30]

Looking back, my life divides pretty cleanly into before Basie and after. The growth I experienced during those years—artistically and professionally—changed everything. Working with Basie was a boot camp. From the first night on the bandstand, I was learning—about music, about discipline, about what it means to show up prepared and present.

It wasn't just skill-building. It was immersion. Life on the road had its own rules and expectations—from the bandstand to the production crews, to the audiences who expected you to deliver every single night. I was learning how the whole ecosystem worked.

Seven years later, I left with confidence. I knew how to create opportunities, and I wanted to see what else was possible. I also wanted something new—roots. Phoenix made sense. My wife, Sydney Blaine, had made it her home, and every time I passed through between tours or worked my regular gig at The Nuance in Los Angeles, Phoenix felt welcoming and familiar.

Having a permanent address changed things. It opened doors I couldn't have walked through while living out of a suitcase. I started thinking seriously about how to build a life—and a career—in one place. I kept remembering the teachers from my Detroit childhood: musicians first, educators by calling, whose names were on marquees even while they were shaping young lives during the day.

That became my roadmap. Around 1988–89, I knocked on the door of the Phoenix Union High School District and landed my first contract at Camelback High, teaching guitar and music

---

30 Basie and Murray, *Good Morning Blues,* p 385

theory. That's how it began—not with a grand plan, but with curiosity, initiative, and a willingness to try something new.

~~~

One spring, I filled in for a band instructor on maternity leave for a few months. The final concert would be under my baton. The students had already been working on Gustav Holst's *Jupiter* from *The Planets*—seven movements of beauty and complexity. Fortunately, my classical training meant I knew the score well.

These kids were serious musicians. Some were aiming for college scholarships, and their parents were deeply invested. Along with *Jupiter*, we programmed Holst's *Mars*—ambitious choices, but intentional ones. This was the kind of repertoire that could open doors for young players.

Everything was lining up.

Until it wasn't.

On the night of the spring concert, check-in time came and went. Warm-ups started. And the bass chair was empty.

We waited. We asked around. Someone tried calling the home. No answer.

And suddenly, every conductor's quiet nightmare set in: How do you perform without a bass player?

The show had to go on. But my mind was racing. Where was this kid? Was he safe? A car accident crossed my mind. Family trouble? Something worse?

If I could've played bass, I would've grabbed it and jumped in. But I was the sub—with piano chops, a little flute scat, and a baton in my hand. I kept thinking, can I somehow scat the bass line and hold this thing together?
~~~

Holst was probably spinning somewhere. Hopefully, he forgave us.

The kids did what young musicians do in a crisis—they listened harder than they ever had before. Eyes locked on me. Searching for cues. Looking for a way out. I conducted with my whole body, trying to signal pulse and continuity, hoping sheer will could stand in for missing low end.

We muddled through. Later, we were told most of the audience never noticed. There weren't many classically trained ears in the room. But on that stage? We felt every missing beat.

It turned out the bass player had been dealing with serious trouble at home. I've kept that story confidential ever since. What stays with me isn't the musical scramble—it's the human part. And I still hear from some of those students today. They pop up on Facebook now and then, and it always makes my day.

<p style="text-align:center">~~~</p>

While I was teaching in Phoenix, I also performed musicals, community theater, concerts. Staying active onstage mattered to me. That's how I became involved with Carol MacLeod[31] and helped get Herberger Theater off the ground. I appeared in its first production, *The Time of Your Life*, playing piano and delivering lines. It was playful, alive—and it launched a new chapter for me.

But the foundation for that work had been laid earlier, back in Detroit, during my pre-Basie years teaching at Munger Junior High while doing theater at night. That's where my thespian

---

31 *Carol MacLeod was a longtime Phoenix theater director and educator whose work helped shape the city's modern performing arts community, mentoring generations of local actors.* For biographical background, see "Carol MacLeod," *Phoenix Theater History*, accessed December 6, 2025, https://phoenixtheater-history.com/crew/carol-macleod/.

chops were truly shaped—by talented professionals who took the work seriously and expected you to do the same.

One of the highlights of that time was working with the brilliant Dorothy Ashby[32] in a musical she and her husband created called *3–6–9*. I played a tamale vendor, strolling through the audience singing a song she wrote just for that moment. It was electric—pure theater magic.

Then came *Porgy and Bess* at the Music Hall downtown. I knew the music by heart—we'd worn out the album at home—but the role I wanted wasn't meant to be. Someone from out of town was cast. That happens. You keep moving.

Phoenix's theater scene kept growing, and so did my involvement. I worked with Arizona Community Theater and Phoenix Theater. I played Judas in *Jesus Christ Superstar* before Herberger had its current home. Some of my favorite roles followed—Papa Ge in *Once on This Island*, Billy Flynn in *Chicago*, Jim in *Big River*, and Blue in *Blue*.

Those casts became lifelong friends. You learn quickly who can really sing, who can act, and—most importantly—who can show up and deliver.

~~~

You don't always know, at first, when you're standing at the edge of something important.

---

32 Dorothy Ashby (1932–1986) was a pioneering Detroit-born jazz harpist and composer whose innovative approach brought the concert harp into mainstream jazz. A Cass Technical High School and Wayne State University alumna, she became known for her rhythmic, blues-inflected style and later for influential studio work with artists such as Stevie Wonder and Earth, Wind & Fire. Her boundary-pushing creativity extended beyond jazz into theater projects, including the collaborative musical *3-6-9*.
~~~

Sometimes it doesn't announce itself. No drumroll. No spotlight. It starts quietly—maybe with a phone call, or a rehearsal schedule, or a flight to a city where you'll be living out of a suitcase for a while. Tucson, in this case.

When they reached out to me about *Blue*, I knew I could do it well.

Not out of bravado—out of recognition. I understood the life. I understood the music. I understood that love songs are seductive by design, and that a jazz singer lives in the space between longing and truth. That's where *Blue* lives.

Before rehearsals even began, most of us went to Pasadena to see the production. We watched carefully. Not to imitate—but to understand the bones of it. Then we settled in for longer-term rehearsals in Tucson. Long enough that it stopped feeling like a tour stop and started feeling like a temporary life. Some nights in a hotel. Some nights in the homes of patrons who loved the theater enough to open their doors to artists they barely knew.

That kind of generosity stays with you. It creates a responsibility to the work.

This wasn't a show you could fake your way through.

While it was categorized as a comedy, everyone involved understood the unspoken rule: comedy is built on truth. And the truth at the center of *Blue* is disruption. I played *Blue*—the jazz singer whose presence, and whose affair with the married matriarch Mrs. Clark, unsettles the internal order of a well-appointed family and exposes fault lines that were already there.

Blue is the catalyst. The centrifugal force. The change agent.

That role asks you to be grounded, seductive without being showy, confident without being cruel. It requires listening as much as singing. And that came naturally to me—not because I was acting like a jazz singer, but because I was one.

The preparation was intense, but not in the loud way people imagine. It was quiet intensity. Listening. Adjusting. Finding the pocket where your voice belongs next to someone else's. Learning when not to sing. Learning when to let silence do the work.

And then there was my leading lady.

I wasn't star struck per se—but I was curious. Curious about what I might learn from her. Actors credit one another for the ways we help each other grow, professionally and personally. That curiosity keeps you open.

For some readers, especially younger ones, her name may not land immediately. So here are a few clues.

She was part of one of the most watched television events in American history—Roots—a cultural touchstone that reshaped how this country talked about race, history, and family. She won a Tony Award before many of today's performers were born. Broadway, television, music, film—she had done it all.

By the time we met, we both knew who was standing in the room.

When the director shared everyone's credentials early on, I had no doubt she'd heard I'd sung with Basie, and about the other theatrical work I'd done. That mattered—not for ego, but for trust. She knew I had chops. I knew she did. From there, the work could begin.

Working alongside this leading lady reinforced something I've always believed: true professionals don't dominate the stage— they elevate it. She was humble. Kind. Experienced in a way that never tipped into ego. Every choice she made served the piece.

And I paid attention.

I've been told over the years that I'm coachable. I laugh at that, because in some areas of life I may not be. But in a rehearsal room? Absolutely. Especially one like that.

I watched. I listened. I absorbed every nuance and styling she brought to our shared moments. Being her counterpart on that stage—night after night—was a privilege. I relished every bit of it.

After Tucson, Arizona Theatre Company carried the production to Phoenix. Then we moved on to Coconut Grove, Florida. Later, the journey continued (without me) to Paper Mill Playhouse—a storied American stage with a deep theatrical history.[33]

We all knew early on that we had something special.

The production earned an award nomination. We didn't win. But awards were never the point.

You don't do these roles for trophies.

You do them for the process. For the music. For the truth that unfolds in real time. For the feeling when an audience recognizes itself in a story—sometimes laughing, sometimes silent, sometimes uncomfortably so.

Years later, what stays with me isn't applause.

It's the way we worked together. The way respect moved quietly through the room.The way the story trusted us to tell it honestly.

It was Blue's raw haunting, melodic lines I'll never forget singing to her character, Peggy Clark. The cast understood how these lyrics and their truth eerily resonated, and it gave me chills during every performance:

---

33 History," *Paper Mill Playhouse*, accessed January 2026, https://papermill.org/about-us/history-2/.

"Sometimes the winds of change blow your way,
you can choose to stay and face the thing
Sometimes you don't know why you were called
To stand for something all for one and one for all."[34]

So if I were to introduce my leading lady now, the way that moment deserves, I'd do it the only way that feels right.

Ladies and gentlemen… Leslie Uggams—whose name is music to our ears; whose heart has made ours flourish and flutter through her leading-lady roles[35]; and whose vitality and voice have shaped the stage and screen soundtracks of American life, for as long as many of us can remember.

~~~

Aside from all the playhouses and theatre stages I've enjoyed, there is one, Phoenix's The Nash, that encourages the musicians to really connect and reach, and where I still play with others. It is a great place to host my student recitals—a venue where Basie's point is part of its very essence and reminds all, "You can still be yourself and keep up with the times."

The jam sessions, the families, the unexpected reunions. People come in and say, "You don't remember me, but I was in your choir," or "You gave me my first solo." I see students from thirty years ago and think, "Man, you grew up good!"

The Nash gives me something back every time I'm there.

---

34 Lyrics from *Blue*, a play by Charles Randolph-Wright, with music by Nona Hendryx and lyrics by Hendryx and Randolph-Wright. Dennis Rowland performed the role of Blue; the role of Peggy Clark was played by Leslie Uggams.
35 "Harlem's Leslie Uggams, Lynn Whitfield and Others Are Blue at the Apollo Theater," Harlem World Magazine, accessed January 2026, https://www.harlemworldmagazine.com/harlems-leslie-uggams-lynn-whitfield-and-others-are-blue-at-the-apollo-theater/.
~~~

Gifted jazz ladies and icons, Hope Morgan[36] Diana Lee[37] Delphine Cortez and Francine Reed[38]—jazz Divas at birth I'm privileged to do sets with and who regularly invite me to play around town. And yeah — I played Ravenscroft last May with the New Guard Big Band which focuses. "primarily on the works of Count Basie and his Orchestra." This 17-piece ensemble is ardently managed and rehearsed by my good friend, Kevin Tangney, and "is a musical freight train full of swagger and swing."[39] That was a thrill. Wonderful familiar faces all around.

Kids who've gone through Scottsdale Community College and now play professionally—they aren't kids anymore and many are established music instructors around the state. Seeing them in these bands and at gigs, it's a fantastic walk down memory lane. Today, when this wide network of jazz and thespian

36 Hope Morgan is a Phoenix-based jazz vocalist, arranger, and educator known for her long-time collaborations with leading musicians in the region. She performs regularly with pianist Nicole Pesce and has been a musical colleague and supporter of Dennis Rowland for decades. A native New Yorker, Hope Morgan arrived in Austin's jazz scene in the mid 1980s. She's learned from such jazz greats as Archie Shepp, Stanley Cowell, Ken McIntyre and Max Roach. In Austin, she worked with the late Gene Ramey upon his re-emergence to the jazz scene. In 1995 the City of Austin declared June 8, 1995 Hope Morgan Day. That year, she was also named Best Female Jazz Vocalist by the Austin Jazz Players and Critics Poll. See Hope Morgan https://womeninjazz.org/performer/hope-morgan/, accessed (12-12-2025)

37 Diana Lee is an Arizona vocalist, vocal coach, and session singer whose career spans jazz, pop, R&B, and gospel. A longtime friend and collaborator of Dennis Rowland, she has recorded and performed widely, including commercial and studio vocal work, and has served as a mentor to many emerging singers in the Phoenix community. Dennis credits Diana with helping him rehabilitate through the use of his music and music therapy to the level where he can still perform today after his stroke.
See "Diana Lee," *Marmoset Music*, accessed [month day, year], https://www.marmosetmusic.com/artists/diana-lee.

38 https://cabaretscenes.org/2025/03/20/delphine-cortez-hope-morgan-francine-reed-the-valley-jazz-divas-show/

39 "The New Guard Big Band," *Upcoming Events*, Mesa Community College Performing Arts Center, accessed January 2026, https://www.upcomingevents.com/mesa/events/mcc-performing-arts-center/the-new-guard-big-band-567722.

buds get together at the pre-shows, in the lobbies or the dressing rooms, it's like a grand reunion. We love to create music together—music that's pure jazz and a joy to share. For the jazzophile, this is what bliss is.

In my becoming an honorary Phoenician, as my local friends refer to me, I believe it could not have been realized until I was finally able to stay in one place long enough to call home.

Staying rooted didn't stop my growth—it made it possible. Basie was right: you can still be yourself and grow and keep up with the times.

CHAPTER 8

Gratitude as the Final Measure of Success

"Count my blessings... I've been very lucky."
— Count Basie

"I've been blessed . . . I never sit down to a meal without first pausing to give thanks. Fate has been very good to me and I'm thankful."[40]

This was Basie's final note: gratitude. He measured his success not just by his career, but by the years spent doing what he loved with people he respected. "Every time I think about how many years I've been able to do what I enjoy doing and make a pretty good living and also make a name for myself and a reputation that stands for something, I realize how much I have to be grateful for."[41]

For those who followed his career, they know that his health in the waning years was a challenge. He pared back our performances to help balance his recovery time from some ailments that required him to stay at home and rehabilitate.

One of those hiatuses led to his adoption of a motor scooter that allowed him to approach the stage, then one of the band managers would help him walk to the piano. Folks, I can relate, I have had my own health challenges and like Basie said,

---

40 Basie and Murray, *Good Morning Blues,* p. 384
41 *Ibid.*

". . . when you hit your seventies, you can't really expect to feel in tip-top condition every day, anyway. So, you just hang on in there, and you go on out and make the gig, and you feel much better doing that than you do just lying around worrying about yourself."[42]

~~~

I don't remember everything about that day, but I remember enough[43]. December 19, 2012. I was driving to a Christmas rehearsal at Asbury United Methodist Church—holiday traffic, people darting around, the usual Phoenix chaos—and all of a sudden, as I've told people many times now, *"it got stupid."* Something was wrong. I knew it immediately. I felt myself slipping, the world tilting just a hair off center.

But I kept the car steady. That's the part that still amazes the doctors: somehow, I navigated through that mess of traffic, signaled, stayed in my lane, and made it to the church parking lot. The performer in me—the one raised in Detroit, trained by the best, polished by Basie—came up for air one more time.

The first words out of my mouth were, "I don't think I can sing today, because I'm having a little problem." Understatement of the century.

That was it. That was the last moment before the lights went out.

I slipped into a coma in the parking lot. Four days later, I woke up at St. Joseph's—Joe's, as we all call it—at the Barrow Neurological Institute. That place saved my life. The doctors later told me I had suffered a severe stroke and a cerebral hemor-

---

42   Basie and Murray, Good Morning Blues, p. 378

43   Jason P. Woodbury, *"Dennis Rowland Returns After Near-Fatal Stroke,"* Phoenix Magazine, July 2015, https://www.phoenixmag.com/2015/07/01/dennis-rowland-returns-after-near-fatal-stroke/
~~~

rhage. I had been, in my own words, "real far out there." They weren't sure I was coming back.

But I did. Slowly.

When I "came out of the fog," as I like to say, and realized I was still here on this earth, my mind went straight to the two constants in my life: singing, and basketball. I didn't think about death, or fear, or what-ifs. I thought about music, and I thought about shooting a jumper. So the first thing I did was hum—just a little scale, nothing fancy. *"Just to see what that was,"* I tell people, I didn't dare try words yet; I just needed to know if the machinery still worked.

Then I raised my hand and moved my wrist through the air, like I was flicking up a basketball. Even now, more than a decade later, that moment still chokes me up. The simplest movements—humming, shooting—felt like a miracle.

The diagnosis came next: aphasia and apraxia. Big, heavy words. Hard words. Words that meant I could think but not say; that I could feel the line of a phrase but not push it cleanly out of my mouth. For a singer, that's a frightening mirror. I spent Christmas in the ICU, New Year's just learning how to begin again.

And then the work started.

People talk about rehabilitation like it's a set of appointments: physical therapy, speech therapy, daily exercises. But it's a whole other thing to live inside that grind. It's humbling. It's slow. It tests you. And I owe a debt of gratitude—one I can never fully repay—to the therapists who showed up for me every day, who pushed me, who coaxed words out of my stubborn mouth, who refused to let me give up when I got tired or frustrated. And of course, my wife, Sydney who was beside me throughout.

They saw the singer in me before I was willing to believe he was still there.

My speech therapist made me work harder than I've ever worked on any stage. My physical therapists made it their mission to get me back on my feet, back to my rhythm, back to the breath and posture and strength a vocalist needs. They didn't just help me recover—they handed me the tools to rebuild myself.

It took a while before I sang publicly again. Father's Day, 2013, Scottsdale Plaza Resort. I wasn't ready for full-on lyrics with complicated tongue twisters, so with a lot of help from my friends, especially Joel Robin Goldenthal, Felix Sainz and Diana Lee, I scatted and sang *All Blues*, which has very simple lyrics. Purposefully, I needed this selection to be the bridge for building back my confidence.

The sea
The sky
And you and I
Sea and sky and you and I
We're all blues
All shades
All hues
All blues

It's funny—scatting had always been something I did for the joy of it, leaning into the horns, sliding around the band like a good tenor player. But that day, it was survival. It was proof. It was me saying, out loud and in front of people: *I'm still here.*

"I knew all the music; music was not a problem," I told someone later. "My problem is the words. Not what they are—but how to say them."

That was the truth. My brain knew every tune, every bit of phrasing, every harmonic turn. But the road from memory to mouth had been blown out. So we rebuilt it, brick by brick.

Thirteen (lucky) years have passed now. And let me tell you—time has been generous.

I'm still teaching at Scottsdale Community College, working with students whose energy keeps me young, whose dreams light the room. I tell them the same thing Celeste Cole and every other great teacher told me: your gift is yours, but your discipline is what carries you. I owe it to them to pour into them the way my mentors poured into me—especially after my stroke, reminding me how fragile and precious all of this is.

I'm back on the bandstand, too. Regular nights at The Nash. Beautiful nights at the Ravenscroft, especially with the younger lions of the New Guard Band. Those guys cook. They keep me honest. They listen, they ask questions, they swing with joy. Singing with them is like opening a window and letting new air rush in.

And yes, I'm still singing the standards—the songs I grew up loving, the songs I sang with Basie, the songs that carried me across the world. These days I sing them with more gratitude, more humor, and more patience for myself. Some nights the words still make me work. Some nights they fall right into place. Either way, I step into the music with reverence.

When I perform now, I think of the night years ago at Mesa Arts Center, when Bruce Gates brought me onstage as a surprise guest. The applause that rolled toward me felt like a welcome home. I remember walking out there, dressed sharp, just happy to be upright and singing again. And when it was over—when the band cooked and the crowd roared and the cameras flashed—I leaned over to the pianist, Nick Manson, and whispered with a little grin:

"See how easy that was?"

A joke. A lie. A truth. All at once. Because none of this has been easy. But it has been worth every second.

I'm still singing. Still teaching. Still lifting weights and shooting baskets at The Village. Still getting onstage with friends, still finding new music to love, still grateful—deeply grateful—for the second chance I was given.

People sometimes ask me if I'm done.

No. I'm not done.

Coda

People often ask whether a place makes a person—or whether a person simply rises above their surroundings. After living nearly eight decades inside music, teaching, travel, and community, I've come to believe the answer is not either/or. A place doesn't make a person alone—but it can *shape the rhythm they learn to live by*.

Detroit shaped mine.

It gave me sound before language, harmony before ambition, and mentorship before ego. It taught me that music was not something you pursued alone, but something you entered into—with others, for others. Long before I ever stepped onto a stage with Count Basie, I was already learning what it meant to belong to something larger than myself.

That lesson followed me everywhere.

When I joined Count Basie's Orchestra in 1977, I did not yet have the words for what I was witnessing. I only knew how it *felt*. Night after night, city after city, there was a steadiness to the music and to the man at the piano. Basie did not lead by force, volume, or spectacle. He led by *holding the center*—by keeping the band together, by honoring each voice and instrument, and by creating an environment where excellence felt natural, expected, and shared.

Years later, when I read his autobiography *Good Morning Blues*, I realized what I had lived without naming it. In the book, Albert Murray described Basie's secret plainly: *"There's an element of the band as an extension of family life—of a very special kind of togetherness."* Thad Jones said it even more vividly, calling it *"a strong and binding family circle... concern for each other's welfare... consistently maintained."* That, he said, was Basie's true genius. I saw that genius up close.

Basie understood that leadership is not about standing apart—it's about *staying present.* He listened. He trusted. He gave people room to grow without ever letting the center fall apart. The band swung because the relationships did. The music worked because the human structure beneath it was sound.

Those lessons did not end when I left the band.

They followed me into classrooms, rehearsal halls, jam sessions, theaters, churches, and community colleges. They shaped the way I teach, the way I listen, the way I try to create space for others to find their voice. I learned that mentorship is not about imprinting yourself on someone else—it's about helping them discover who they already are and giving them the discipline to honor it.

If this book has a purpose beyond memory, it is this: to pass on what was so generously passed to me.

Keeping the beat, as I've come to understand it, is not only a musical responsibility. It is a human one. It means showing up. It means holding time for others. It means sustaining a culture where people feel seen, supported, and challenged to be their best selves—together.

To this day, I remember that bond.

I feel it every time performers, former students, and now bandleaders—our alumni—find one another in dressing rooms, hotel lobbies, venue hallways, and after-parties. I don't need to *apply* those principles consciously when I see the gang.

They're already there. We're family—bound by the love of jazz and by the shared understanding that we created something worth carrying forward for the next generation to build upon.

That is Basie's legacy.

And it is the beat I will keep, for as long as I'm able.

Frequently Asked Questions

Over the years, interviewers have often asked similar questions about my past and my experiences in the industry. For fun, I've compiled a list that captures most of them.

Q. What is your heritage and where does your family come from?

According to Ancestry.com, my people come from Nigeria, Western Bantu Peoples and Benin and Togo. This was fascinating to learn. I should add, for a little color, that the smallest percentages of my line were traced to northeast Scotland, Denmark and northwest Germany

Q. Your grandfather lived with your family in Detroit. Had he been a slave?

No, he was born in the 1880s, twenty years after Emancipation. I assumed his father and mother were, but do not have the memory of his telling me stories about that.

History would have it that my great grandparents on both sides were enslaved. Their children moved north during the Great Migration taking them ultimately to Detroit from Mississippi and Georgia.

My grandfather, my father's father, aged gradually and gently as I grew up. He was kind, thoughtful and understood how to amuse the little kid in me. Some of my fondest memories are of the two of us watching from our second-floor breezeway area, the construction of the freeway adjacent to our home. The earthmovers, cranes and construction noise outside our two-family flat was prevalent for a time.

As a youngster, but especially later as I was able to physically support his weight, I would help with his bathing and getting around the home as he became less able.

Q. How many children and grandchildren do you have?

One daughter who has two grown children. Between those two grandchildren, I have six great grandchildren.

Q: How did you meet Sydney, your wife now of more than 30 years?

I met Syd in 1980 while performing with the Count Basie Orchestra in Tokyo. She was living in Hawaii then. We married in 1995, coinciding with the launch of my solo recording career. Her love and support for me is unwavering and has been the foundation for my post-touring years, including my recovery from the near-fatal stroke in 2012. She was by my side through that recovery and has been a strong, loving influence in my life.

Q: What are the large-ensemble recordings you made during your tenure with the Count Basie Orchestra? Why were Basie singers rarely foregrounded on albums?

When people ask me what I recorded with the Count Basie Orchestra, I always have to explain that being a Basie singer was less about making "vocal albums" and more about being part of a working band—night after night, city after city. The recordings that document my time with Basie are large-ensemble recordings that reflect the orchestra's *touring life*, not spotlight projects built around a singer.

During my tenure in the late 1970s and early 1980s, that working sound was captured on recordings such as:

Basie, Count, and His Orchestra. *On the Road*. Pablo Records, 1980. LP.
Basie, Count, and His Orchestra. *Kansas City Shout*. Pablo

Records, 1980. LP.

Basie, Count, and His Orchestra. *The Last Concert*. Pablo Records, recorded 1980, released 1981. LP.

Those albums weren't designed to feature a vocalist front and center. They were documents of how the band *functioned*—how it swung, how it breathed, how it carried Basie's time from one night to the next.

That's also why Basie singers were rarely foregrounded on albums. Count Basie believed the orchestra itself was the star. Singers were an essential part of the texture—another instrument in the ensemble—but never the point of emphasis. Vocals came and went naturally, just like a trumpet solo or a tenor chorus, and then the band kept moving.

Onstage, that made you incredibly disciplined. You learned to respect space, to tell a story quickly, to swing without stepping on the band. Basie didn't want singers who *stood in front* of the orchestra—he wanted singers who *rode inside it*. That philosophy didn't always translate into liner notes or track listings, but it taught me everything I know about timing, restraint, and leadership.

In a Basie band, if you were doing your job right, the music always came first—and your name came second.

Q. You played for several years at the Nuance in Los Angeles with Gregg Field[44]. The Nuance was a frequented place for LA talent, famous names and faces. What kind of opportunities arose from that long-time gig?

When I moved to Phoenix and began the easy commute to Los Angeles, one of the most important musical relationships of my life was with Gregg Field who was based there. For a number

---

44 Gregg Field is a Los Angeles–based jazz drummer and producer whose long-running collaboration with Dennis Rowland at the Nuance led to multiple recordings and helped define Rowland's post–Count Basie artistic direction. Field and Rowland played in the new testament Basie band.

of years, Gregg and I held down a regular gig at The Nuance, a small but legendary room that quietly drew the city's deepest musical talent—and more than a few famous faces who loved jazz and wanted to be close to it.

The Nuance wasn't about hype. It was about *listening*. Night after night, we played for musicians, actors, writers—people who knew the music and respected the craft. Because of that, opportunities didn't come in the form of auditions or contracts handed across a table. They came as conversations. Introductions. Trust built over time.

One of those relationships was with Dabney Coleman. Dabney was already an Emmy-winning actor—*9 to 5*, *Tootsie*, *On Golden Pond*—and to us, he was simply a genuine jazz lover and a loyal friend. He believed in what Gregg and I were doing and stepped in as a supporter and producer for the albums we made together. Having Dabney in our corner wasn't just helpful, it was affirming. It told us the work mattered beyond the room, beyond the moment.

Those Nuance years gave me something invaluable: artistic freedom. Gregg and I had the space to explore repertoire, develop a shared language, and record music that reflected who we really were—not trends, not expectations. What grew out of that long-time gig were albums, yes—but more than that, a musical identity rooted in trust, patience, and respect for the song.

Q. What were the pieces you performed for your Kentucky State scholarship audition and for your Basie tryouts?

Our high school choir went to Kentucky State and I auditioned for acceptance with Handel's *Where 'er You Walk* and Hammerstein's *You'll Never Walk Alone.*

For the Basie tryouts, I sang *Everyday* and a couple of other standards to show some versatility—but I don't recall now. My friendship and performing years with Jimmy Wilkins'

Big Band was certainly an advantage. Jimmy, who had played with Basie long before I did, and whose renowned saxophonist brother arranged Basie and Williams' *Everyday*, had the charts from those Basie years. Jimmy, at the time of my tryout, was the band director at Northwestern High School, the band I borrowed for the tryout, and was a highly revered instructor.

I was elated when Kentucky State offered me a full scholarship and so were my parents. Looking back now, I would probably say I was sought after by Kentucky State. But I also did a couple of other auditions with the same pieces for Eastern Michigan and Michigan State. But in both instances, in the back of my mind, I didn't think I would be going to those places because they didn't compare to what Kentucky State could do for a kid like me from Detroit. The large lecture hall experience wasn't what I needed or wanted.

Having spent my formative years in music with piano and voice lessons, I had spent a lot of time performing as a young student and loved doing it. But, I really was raw talent and had a lot to learn. College helped cultivate it through incredible teachers who were bigtime performers themselves.

Q. There is a little-known story about the two Dr. Smith's in your life, both at Kentucky State and decidedly influential in your collegiate growth and bridging into your first gig. Care to tell us a bit about these gifted gents and how they touched your life?

Dr. Carl Smith and Dr. Lewis Smith. The Smiths, not brothers, not related but certainly bookends for me during the college years. First, Dr. Carl Smith was *the* revered professor of music (or in the role that reflected that responsibility) and his pedigree was impeccable. He provided just the kind of coaching, insight and direction I needed throughout my time at the University. I was in awe of him, as were all the other music students.

Second, Dr. Lewis Smith was also an academic and he was the

gent who helped me get my first gig as an upperclassman in college—in Louisville. The memories proliferating my brain are of Dr. Lewis driving us in his shiny fire-engine-red Cadillac from Frankfort to Louisville, and what should have taken us a couple of hours—only took us one hour.

That Caddy and Dr. Lewis Smith were a smokin hot rocket going down the highway. Never got pulled over. The guys and I'd laugh in disbelief that we were goin about 90-100 mph and Dr. Smith had one hand on the wheel, talking and carrying on like we were sittin at a bar chewin' the fat. Unbelievable.

The gig?

Joe's Palm Room.[45]

---

45 Joe's Palm Room was a historically Black-owned nightclub in Louisville that played a central role in the city's mid-20th-century jazz and R&B scene, hosting touring national acts and serving as a vital cultural gathering place. After decades of closure, the venue has recently reopened, reclaiming its legacy as a landmark of Black musical entrepreneurship and community life. See Leo Weekly, "Joe's Palm Room: A Legendary Black-Owned Club in Louisville Is Back," Leo Weekly, accessed January 26, 2026, https://www.leoweekly.com/food-drink/joes-palm-room-a-legendary-black-owned-club-in-louisville-is-back-15765148/

Discography

What follows is a record of the music behind the story, beginning with the rigor of the Count Basie Orchestra and tracing Dennis Rowland's development as a jazz vocalist from large-ensemble work to the collaborative years in which his voice emerged fully on his own terms. The recordings include projects released on major jazz labels, including Concord and Capitol, as well as independent and guest-featured work shaped by his Los Angeles and Phoenix years. (Vocalist credits on large-ensemble recordings are often collective rather than track-specific.)

Dennis also contributed vocals to Ray Anthony's *Swings the Thing*, a boxed set celebrating his music with the Verve acoustic series, where Dennis appears on select tracks.

With the Count Basie Orchestra
(Late 1970s–Early 1980s: Touring and large-ensemble recordings)
Basie, Count, and His Orchestra. *On the Road*. Pablo Records, 1980. LP.
Grammy Award for Best Jazz Instrumental Performance, Big Band (1981). Includes "Work Song" (Nat Adderley and Oscar Brown Jr.), featuring Dennis Rowland, vocalist.
Basie, Count, and His Orchestra. *Kansas City Shout*. Pablo Records, 1980. LP.
Basie, Count, and His Orchestra. *The Last Concert*. Pablo Records. Recorded 1980; released 1981. LP.

Major-Label and Studio Recordings
(Concord and Capitol years; leader and featured vocalist)
Rowland, Dennis. *Rhyme, Rhythm & Reason*. Concord Records, 1990s. CD.Produced by Dabney Coleman.
Rowland, Dennis. *Get Here*. Concord Records, 1990s. CD.
Rowland, Dennis. *Now Dig This*. Concord Records, 1990s. CD.
A celebration of 1950s and early 1960s Miles Davis repertoire.

Los Angeles Years: Collaborations with Gregg Field
(Long-running engagement at the Nuance; duo and small-ensemble recordings)
Rowland, Dennis, and Gregg Field. *I Can't Believe You're in Love with Me*. Sea Breeze Jazz, 1994. CD
Rowland, Dennis, and Gregg Field. *This Is New*. Sea Breeze Jazz, 1997. CD.

Guest Appearances and Featured Recordings
Rowland, Dennis. *Blonde*. Playboy Jazz, n.d. CD.
Inaugural release for the Playboy Jazz label.
Sample, Joe Sample. *Sample This*. Capitol Records, n.d. CD.
Featuring Dennis Rowland, vocals.
Foster, Frank Foster, and the Loud Minority Band. *We Do It Diff'rent*. n.d. CD.
Featuring Dennis Rowland, vocals.
Anthony, Ray. *Swings the Thing*. Boxed set. Verve Records (Acoustic Sounds Series), n.d. CD.
Featuring guest vocals by Dennis Rowland on select tracks.

Guest Appearances and Live Performances
Throughout his career, Dennis Rowland has appeared as a featured guest vocalist with regional and national big bands, jazz orchestras, and educational ensembles, documented through live concerts, broadcasts, and archival recordings rather than commercial studio releases.

References

Ashby, Dorothy. *Selected Recordings and Performances.* Detroit and Los Angeles, 1957–1986.

Harlem World Magazine. "*Harlem's Leslie Uggams, Lynn Whitfield and Others Are Blue at the Apollo Theater.*" Accessed January 2026. https://www.harlemworldmagazine.com/harlems-leslie-uggams-lynn-whitfield-and-others-are-blue-at-the-apollo-theater/

Baldwin, James. *Collected Essays.* Edited by Toni Morrison. New York: Library of America, 1998.

Basie, Count, and Albert Murray. *Good Morning Blues: The Autobiography of Count Basie.* New York: Random House, 1985.

BluesKC.org. *Kansas City Blues History.* Accessed August 15, 2025. https://blueskc.org/kc-blues-history/

"Carol MacLeod." *Phoenix Theater History.* Accessed February 15, 2025. https://phonixtheaterhistory.com/crew/carol-macleod/.

Celeste G. Cole." *Find A Grave.* Accessed [insert date you accessed it]. https://www.findagrave.com/memorial/217999598/celeste_g-cole

Leo Weekly. "Joe's Palm Room: A Legendary Black-Owned Club in Louisville Is Back." *Leo Weekly.* Accessed January 26, 2026. https://www.leoweekly.com/food-drink/joes-palm-room-a-legendary-black-owned-club-in-louisville-is-back-15765148/

Miller, Tom. "The Abyssinian Baptist Church – 132 West 138th Street." *Daytonian in Manhattan.* November 30, 2022. https://daytoninmanhattan.blogspot.com/2022/11/the-abyssinian-baptist-church-132-west.html.

Randolph-Wright, Charles. *Blue.* Music by Nona Hendryx. Lyrics by Nona Hendryx and Charles Randolph-Wright. Performance featuring Dennis Rowland as Blue and Leslie Uggams as Peggy Clark.

Richards, Johnny, and Carolyn Leigh. *Young at Heart.* Recorded by Frank Sinatra. Capitol Records, 1953.

Stryker, Mark. *Jazz from Detroit.* Ann Arbor: University of Michigan Press, 2019.

United Press International. "Funeral Services Were Held Today for Jazz Great Count...." *UPI Archives.* April 30, 1984. https://www.upi.com/Archives/1984/04/30/Funeral-services-were-held-today-for-jazz-great-Count/9264452145600/

United Press International. "Hundreds of Admirers Lined a Funeral Home Sunday to…." *UPI Archives*. April 29, 1984. https://www.upi.com/Archives/1984/04/29/Hundreds-of-admirers-lined-a-funeral-home-Sunday-to/5306452062800/.
Upcoming Events. "The New Guard Big Band." Mesa Community College Performing Arts Center. Accessed January 2026. https://www.upcomingevents.com/mesa/events/mcc-performing-arts-center/the-new-guard-big-band-567722
Wilson, John S. "Count Basie, 79, Band Leader and Master of Swing, Dead." *New York Times*, April 27, 1984. https://www.nytimes.com/1984/04/27/arts/count-basie-79-band-leader-and-master-of-swing-dead.html.
Woodbury, Jason P. "*Dennis Rowland Returns After Near-Fatal Stroke.*" *Phoenix Magazine*, July 2015. https://www.phoenixmag.com/2015/07/01/dennis-rowland-returns-after-near-fatal-stroke/.

About the Authors

Photo by Camerawerks

Dennis Rowland is a renowned jazz vocalist, thespian, educator and longtime musical arts performer based in Phoenix, AZ. A former member of the Count Basie Orchestra, he has spent decades on stage and in the classroom, mentoring musicians and sharing the values he learned from one of jazz's great bandleaders. His work reflects a deep belief in listening, collaboration, and the quiet discipline that allows music—and people—to swing.

Photo by Hannah Lorsch

Marla Sheiner is an author, editor, historian and communications professional whose work explores leadership through history, character, and lived experience. A former press secretary to the late U.S. Senator John McCain during his first congressional campaign, she is the author of *McCain's Navy: A Leadership Field Guide* and *The Mingenback Chronicles*. In *Keeping the Beat*, she brings a leadership lens to jazz icon and maverick Bill Basie, helping shape Dennis Rowland's story and the enduring lessons he learned from The Chief.